aircraft illustrated SPECIAL

LIGHTNING

LONDON
IAN ALLAN LTD

ROGER LINDSAY

Contents

First published 1989

ISBN 0 7110 1825 1

Published by Ian Allan Ltd, Shepperton, Surrey; and printed by Ian Allan Printing Ltd at their works at Coombelands in Runnymede, England

Previous page:
A menacing portrait of a No 11 Squadron F6 shows to good effect the Red Top missiles, typically without main fins to minimise stress and reduce drag. Note also the sturdy, stalky main undercarriage, with landing lights neatly incorporated into the doors, the thin 280lb/sq in tyres, depressed all-flying tailplane, and sharp circular air intake lip with Airpass centre-body radome. *John Dunnell*

This page:
A seven-ship formation of No 74's brand new F6s. Early in 1967 the squadron was the first to receive full-production standard aircraft. *MoD via Andy Molland*

ACKNOWLEDGEMENTS
The Author wishes to thank the following Lightning enthusiasts for their considerable help, which is sincerely appreciated:

Alfie M. Alderson; Flt Lt Ian Black; Alan Carlaw; Dugald Cameron; Peter Cooper; Geoff Cruickshank; Gordon Dare (BAe); John Dawkins (MoD); John Dunnell; Ivy Hammill; Michael Hill (CPRO RAF Strike Command); Gerry and Graham Jackson; Paul A. Jackson; John G. Johnson; Richard King; Gunther Kipp; Jon Lake; Fred Martin; Keith Mason; Andy and Hedley Molland; Richard Moore; John Oaten; Sqn Ldr Tony Paxton; Lindsay Peacock; Brian Pickering (MAP); Wally Rouse (BAe); Terry Senior; Flt Lt R. A. Smith; Dave Tuplin; Flt Lt Andy Thomas; Dick Ward; Keith Watson; Ian White.

Front cover:
Lightning farewell — an F6 of No 11 Squadron is seen on one of its last sorties on 13 April 1988. *Allan Burney*

Back cover, top to bottom:
Lightning F1 XM135 'B' is depicted in No 74 Squadron colours in July 1963. The aircraft is now preserved at the Imperial War Museum, Duxford.

Lightning F1A XM171 served with No 56 Squadron from February 1961 until April 1965. It is shown coded 'A' as it would have been seen in July 1963.

Lightning F3 XR749 'DA' carried this special colour scheme to celebrate the Lightning Training Flight's 10th anniversary.

Lightning F6 XS903 became 'BA' with No 11 Squadron in late 1987, with a black fin and spine colour scheme.

Lightning F6 XR770 'AA' gained its red fin and rudder in October 1986 for No 5 Squadron's 21st anniversary of flying Lightnings. Later the following year the red was extended along the spine and wing leading edge.

Lightning F6 XS899 'AA' of No 5 Squadron in the dark grey scheme it wore during 1983.
All pictures courtesy of Dugald Cameron/ Squadron Prints

Introduction

Sheer exhilaration. Sheer performance. The pastoral panorama of expansive East Anglian fields, verdant with thriving young crops, edged with clumps of Constable trees and basking in the misty morning sunshine of early summer, was relentlessly pushed downwards and behind us as we surged forward, increasingly gathering momentum seconds after rotating from Wattisham's runway and headed for the North Sea. Such was our acceleration that even a deft movement of the stick occasioned by the need to make a slight course correction caused an immediate squeezing of the legs as my anti-G suit automatically responded to the induced force of 3Gs. Minutes later, and after exceeding 1,000mph on our way up, we levelled out at 60,000ft, where the sun blazed down through our Perspex canopy from out of a sky which was as dark as indigo velvet. The vehicle which had provided this thrill of a lifetime and transported me so close to Heaven was the greatest British fighter since the Spitfire — the Lightning.

Outstanding. Unique. These two words seem to be the simplest and most appropriate to describe the remarkable Lightning, yet they are at the same time totally inadequate. The Lightning can streak skywards at over 50,000ft/min

almost as soon as it pair of afterburning Rolls-Royce Avon engines have blasted it off the runway. The same engines can push it along effortlessly at 1,500mph on the level at altitude, and propel it to well over 15 miles high in a zoom climb. It is a pilot's aeroplane, responsive and tolerant, yet demanding enough to keep his adrenalin flowing for the full sortie. It is unique in design, in the arrangement of its engines, and in being the first RAF fighter designed from the outset as an integrated weapons system. More than anything, it is unique in being the only supersonic, Mach 2 aircraft of purely British design and manufacture ever to be produced in quantity. Aware of all these things, it comes as something of a shock to realise that more than a third of a century has slipped by since the publication of the first, coarse-screened, photograph in the national newspapers, which signified the début of the prototype Lightning in that first week of August 1954. Throughout the intervening years the Lightning has fulfilled its intended role of air defender with distinction, exceeding everyone's predictions. Only now in 1988 is it at the conclusion of its illustrious career, which will be exceedingly difficult for any successor to eclipse.

Below:
The author, trussed up in Lightning T5 XS422 of Treble One Squadron prior to the thrill of a lifetime sortie from Wattisham on 20 May 1971.

No 11 Squadron F6s taxy in to Coningsby after diversion from Binbrook, the leader's jet wash of wafting kerosene blurring his followers. *John Dunnell*

Origin & Development

That first Lightning photograph was heavily retouched so that neither the wing nor its tell-tale shadow should reveal its unique shape. At that time the aircraft was simply referred to as the English Electric P1, and the reason that the maiden flight of first prototype WG760 from Boscombe Down on 4 August 1954 attracted so much publicity was that here at last was tangibility of the aircraft billed to take the RAF into the realms of supersonic flight. That successful 30min first flight by English Electric's illustrious chief test pilot, Wg Cdr Roland 'Bee' Beamont, represented the tip of a development iceberg which had originated in 1947 when Experimental Requirement 103 was issued for a research aircraft capable of exploring transonic and low supersonic speeds of up to Mach 1.5. English Electric's design, prosaically termed 'Project 1' (hence P1), had the built-in potential to be a combat aircraft, and it met many of the requirements of Air Ministry specification F23/49 for a supersonic day fighter.

The initial P1 design featured wings swept sharply back at 60° and set low on the fuselage. Its two axial-flow engines were arranged one above the other and fed from a simple nose air intake — originally the upper engine was ahead of the lower in contrast to the reverse layout which was adopted when the design was translated into metal. The tailplane, also swept at 60°, was originally low set at the base of the fuselage to prevent transonic pitch-up. However, designers at RAE Farnborough argued that the tail should sit atop the fin, and this was put to the test on the specially constructed low-speed Short SB5. Suffice to say that after 12 months of testing, English Electric's 60° sweep wing and low-set tail were agreed as giving optimum results.

On 1 April 1950 two flight-test prototypes, WG760 and WG763, had been ordered (together with a static-test airframe), to be powered by two Armstrong-Siddeley Sapphire AS-Sa 5 engines, offering 8,100lb dry thrust apiece, later supplemented by more than 2,000lb of reheat thrust. During WG760's third flight, on 11 August 1954, 'Bee' Beamont created history by exceeding Mach 1 in level flight for the first time in a British aircraft, although this was not realised until the following day when the aircraft's speed was accurately computed. While the first P1A (as the type had been designated to avoid confusion with later versions) was employed primarily on performance and handling tests, WG763, which first flew on 18 July 1955, was fitted with some operational kit, including two 30mm Aden cannon in the nose, and later, a 250gal jettisonable ventral auxiliary fuel tank subsequently adopted on most service versions of the aircraft. WG763 also tested a Napier Double Scorpion rocket motor in lieu of the ventral tank. Eventually the P1A

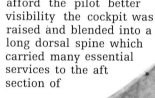

achieved 1,010mph (Mach 1.53) on the level, quite exceptional for such limited engine power, and without autostabilisation it proved to have excellent handling and manoeuvrability.

The P1B was the next step in the evolution to service fighter; it was the first example of the weapons system concept produced by the British aircraft industry, in which the fighter's radar and armament were integrated with the flying controls to provide a single-seat all-weather interceptor, capable of acquiring its target at considerable distances and destroying it with a high degree of certainty — which previously had been the exclusive prerogative of American fighters. In many respects the P1B was very different from the P1A, the most obvious external change being that the oval air intake of the latter was replaced by an annular intake with a fixed, cone-shaped centre body which conveniently housed the Ferranti intercept radar, known as AIRPASS — Airborne Interception Radar Pilot Attack System, or AI23 in service. The Sapphires were replaced by two Rolls-Royce Avons, each developing around 14,000lb thrust with reheat, giving a power-to-weight ratio close to unity. To afford the pilot better visibility the cockpit was raised and blended into a long dorsal spine which carried many essential services to the aft section of

the aircraft. Lateral air brakes were added to each side of the rear fuselage, revised flaps (containing extra fuel) were fitted, and changes were made to the undercarriage, with the main wheels incorporating thin tyres with the incredibly high pressure of 280lb/sq in. A pylon-mounted de Havilland Blue Jay (later Firestreak) infra-red homing missile on each side of the nose was the primary armament. The missiles could be interchanged with alternative packs of either two more Adens or 48 unguided 2in rockets. A slightly taller fin of greater area was also introduced to counteract the reduced stability caused by the two Firestreak missiles.

November 1956 saw initial RAF orders placed, and on 4 April 1957 'Bee' took the first of three P1B prototypes, XA847, on its initial outing, exceeding Mach 1.2 in the process. Coincidentally the government chose the very same day to publish its infamous Defence White Paper in which its architect, Duncan Sandys, stated that the missile era had now dawned and the manned interceptor fighter was soon to become a thing of the past. All of Britain's most promising fighter projects were hastily cancelled, and the P1 was reprieved only because of its advanced stage of development, although it did suffer much reduced orders from those which might otherwise have been anticipated.

On 23 October 1958 the P1B was officially christened the Lightning by the Chief of Air Staff, ending much deliberation during which several other names, including 'Excalibur' had also been proffered. XA847 was used for engine development including testing with the Double Scorpion rocket motor, while the other prototypes, XA853 and XA856, were involved with weapons trials and operational equipment evaluation. This development programme was greatly accelerated by the order for 20 additional pre-production aircraft, a unique and long-overdue departure from previous British practice. Serialled XG307-313 and XG325-337, the first flew on 3 April 1958, powered by RA24R Avons rated at 14,430lb with reheat. During the next few years these pre-production aircraft were engaged in the evolution of the Lightning, testing a variety of features before their incorporation in new marks. One such feature, first tried on XG310, was the enlargement of the fin and rudder by 30%, henceforth to become standard on all 'first generation' Lightnings.

The first of 19 full-production Lightning F1s took to the air on 29 October

Top:
XA847 testing Napier Double Scorpion rocket motors, which conferred exceptional acceleration and the ability to reach altitudes well above 80,000ft. Eventually the scheme was dropped because the Lightning's performance was already more than adequate, without reducing its meagre fuel tankage by the rocket pack!
BAe via Graham Jackson

Above:
XA847 with the extended fin. This aircraft was, until recently, in the RAF Museum, Hendon. Geoff Cruickshank

1959, and December saw the first deliveries of the type to the RAF when XG334-336 of the pre-production batch went to the Air Fighting Development Squadron at Coltishall, Norfolk, when the Lightning received its official release for service use by the Controller, Aircraft.

On 14 May 1960 the RAF took delivery of its first full production F1, XM135 (which also went to the AFDS), and the first operational test for the Lightning came at the end of the same month when six F1s of the AFDS, operating from Leconfield, took part in the annual air defence exercise, 'Yeoman', in which they achieved 'a satisfactory rate of interception'. This rather tongue-in-cheek assessment of their excellent results was probably occasioned by the realisation that serviceability could have been better. Poor serviceability tended to afflict the Lightning during its early service career, including with

No 74 Squadron, which became the first operational squadron to re-equip with the type when XM165 was delivered to Leconfield on 29 June 1960 while the squadron's home base, Coltishall, received attention prior to the introduction of large-scale Lightning operations. The squadron began conversion from its Hunter F6s aided by the AFDS, and it was not until 14 July that a No 74 Squadron pilot — appropriately, the South African CO, Sqn Ldr J. F. G. Howe — flew the Lightning, by which time the squadron was back at Coltishall. Transition from the 720mph Hunter to Mach 2+ Lightning proved surprisingly trouble-free, and 74 was able to demonstrate a quartet of its new supersonic fighters during the Farnborough Air Display in September, operating them from Boscombe Down. By the end of the year it had its full complement of 12 Lightnings and was declared operational early in the New Year.

No 74 remained the only Fighter Command squadron solely equipped with the F1 version of the Lightning, and the first to perform formation aerobatics with the type. In the spring of 1961 the squadron formed a six-ship aerobatic team which gave several displays, including the Paris Air Show in June, and by borrowing four aircraft from the AFDS, 74 was able to increase the team and fly in diamond-nine formation at Farnborough in September. As the 'Tigers', 74 represented Fighter Command during 1962 and gave displays in Sweden and Norway, and just prior to the Farnborough show in September it initiated a colourful era among Lightning squadrons by painting the fins and spines of its aircraft glossy black.

On 28 January 1964 No 74 moved to Leuchars, Fife, where it re-equipped with later Lightnings from April onwards, enabling its F1s to be handed down to second-line training units. In fact 74 had already donated seven F1s to help establish No 226 (Lightning) Operational Conversion Unit which was formed at Middleton-St-George on 1 June 1963 to train prospective Lightning pilots and which later also ran refresher and weapons attack instructor courses. On 13 April 1964 No 226 OCU moved to Coltishall, later acquiring more ex-No 74 Squadron F1s until these were phased out of service early in 1965. Apart from three aircraft lent to No 111 Squadron in 1964, by far the longest spell of service by F1s was as high-speed manned targets, operated

by the Target Facilities Flights at Binbrook (initially part of the Fighter Command Trials Unit), Wattisham, and Leuchars from 1966 until December 1973 when these units were disbanded. Prior to their TFF role these aircraft were updated at No 33 MU, Lyneham, where several F1s were prematurely scrapped in 1965, before No 60 MU at Leconfield took over as the main RAF Lightning storage and major maintenance unit.

The next Lightning variant to see service was the F1A, which differed from its predecessor in possessing an in-flight refuelling capability by virtue of a detachable probe which fitted beneath the port wing, an improved windscreen rain/ice dispersal system, UHF radio instead of VHF, and some revisions to internal equipment and wiring which resulted in the presence of an external cable duct along each side of the lower fuselage — featured on all subsequent marks. The first of 28 F1As, XM169, flew on 16 August 1960, and No 56 Squadron at Wattisham, Suffolk, became the first operational user with its receipt of XM172 on 14 December 1960, followed by No 111 Squadron at the same base in the spring of 1961. The F1A's ability to refuel in flight was extensively practised by these squadrons, and in July 1962 a section of No 56's Lightnings flew non-stop from Wattisham to Akrotiri, Cyprus, taking on fuel from Valiant tankers. In June 1962 No 111 Squadron took part in a redeployment exercise to RAF Germany, and later sent a detachment of aircraft to Malta, which then went on to Libya, where, with Firestreaks replaced by a pack containing an additional pair of Aden cannon, the Lightnings conducted live air-to-ground firing over desert ranges close to their temporary base of El Adem. Meanwhile No 56 Squadron provided Fighter Command's 1963 aerobatic team of Lightnings, named the 'Firebirds' after the unit's phoenix badge; a distinctive colour scheme of scarlet fin, spine, wing and tailplane edges completed the finishing touches to an extremely impressive repertoire. Early in 1965 the Wattisham Wing re-equipped with later Lightnings thereby releasing Lightning F1As for No 226 OCU where they replaced F1s, and later supplemented the TFFs

Thanks to the availability of simulators, a thorough training plan, and the relative experience of those first RAF pilots selected to fly the Lightning, the conversion from subsonic aircraft had gone well, although it was realised at an early stage in the development of the P1B that a dual-controlled trainer variant was desirable. Design of the two-seater, known as the P11, began in the summer of 1957, and the prototype, XL628, flew on 6 May 1959. It was virtually identical to the F1 with the exception that the forward fuselage was widened 11½in to accommodate

Above:
XG313, the seventh pre-production aircraft, with enlarged fin, test firing 2in unguided rockets from the nose weapons pack. *BAe*

Below:
A Salmesbury scene, circa 1959, with Development Batch and early production F1 Lightnings in final assembly. XG326 is behind the World War 2 vintage AEC bowser — illustrating the strides which the aviation industry had made in less than 15 years! *BAe*

Above:
Battle Flight readiness alert sheds (comparable with UK QRA hangars) at RAF Gütersloh, with a brace of No 19 Squadron F2s awaiting the order to scramble. *RAF*

side-by-side seating (then in vogue with RAF trainers), in an enlarged cockpit, partly derived from the two-seat Hunter T7. The changes resulted in the deletion of the upper Aden cannon, but otherwise the Lightning trainer, designated the T4, was as operationally competent as the F1, and only marginally slower. After the first prototype crashed into the Irish Sea on 1 October 1959 flight testing was resumed from the 21st of the month when the second prototype, XL629, first flew. Thirty production T4s (later reduced to 20), based on the F1A rather than the F1, were ordered for the RAF, the first, XM966, flying on 15 July 1960. The Lightning Conversion Squadron became the first recipient on 27 June 1962 when XM970 was delivered to Middleton-St-George. The LCS became No 226 OCU a year later, and adopted the shadow role and markings of No 145 Squadron, until May 1971 when its F1As and T4s changed to those of No 65 Squadron, which remained in vogue until the OCU disbanded at Coltishall in September 1974 when the remaining T4s were scrapped. Operational squadrons flying Mk 1 or 2 fighters each received at least one T4,

the last of which saw service with Nos 19 and 92 Squadrons in Germany. Two former RAF T4s, XM989 and XM992, were transferred to the Royal Saudi Air Force in 1966 with the designation T54.

The fourth Lightning variant to see squadron service was the F2. Externally almost identical to the F1A, beneath its skin lay several important improvements: Avon 210 engines with much needed fully-variable reheat instead of the four-stage reheat of earlier versions; a liquid oxygen system; automatic flight control; improved instrumentation and avionics; and a standby turbo-generator for dc electric supply — the small dorsal intake for this equipment providing the only easy means of identifying the F2 apart from the serial number.

XN723, the first F2 to fly, was airborne on 11 July 1961; but in common with the Lightning production programme in general, an inordinate time elapsed before the first service unit took delivery, when XN771 was handed over to the AFDS at Binbrook on 14 November 1962. Forty-four F2s were ordered, but several were retained on

development work and converted to later marks, so that only two operational squadrons used this mark — Nos 19 and 92 at Leconfield, which re-equipped from Hunters between November 1962 and May 1963. Five former RAF F2s were exported to Saudi Arabia as F52s in 1966/67.

On 23 September 1965 No 19 Squadron moved to Gütersloh to become permanently established in RAF Germany under the control of the 2nd ATAF, NATO. No 92 Squadron followed to Geilenkirchen on 29 December, but joined up again with No 19 at Gütersloh in February 1968. These squadrons maintained a Battle Flight at constant readiness every day in the year, to guard against incursions into Allied air space by Warsaw Pact aircraft based less than 100 miles away. Similarly, pairs of Lightnings in Britain were held on Quick Reaction Alert status 24 hours a day and were frequently scrambled to investigate unidentified aircraft entering the UK Air Defence Identification Zone.

As this manace grew, special QRA 'sheds', housing two aircraft, their pilots and groundcrew, were built at the western end of Lightning base runways. Most of the Soviet incursions were off Northern Scotland, providing Leuchars with by far the most trade and hence priority in re-equipment

9

Above:
XN725, an F2 development aircraft modified to F3A standard with Avon 301 engines.
BAe

with the latest Lightning, the F3. No 74 Squadron took delivery of XP700, the first example to reach an operational squadron, on 14 April 1964.

The F3 was the hottest Lightning of all with more reliable Avon 301s giving a power : weight ratio close to unity, with a corresponding improvement in acceleration and agility — but at the expense of endurance which could cut down a sortie to as short as 35-40min. The F3 was easily identified by its new square-cut fin (first tested on XG310) of 15% increased area, which gave a clue to a major advance in armament — the Red Top missile. In conjunction with new AI23B radar, the Red Top, although derived from the Firestreak, permitted collision-course interception. Avionics were more sophisticated, too, including the installation of OR946 instrumen-

An unusual quartet: a Shackleton AEW2 of No 8 Squadron leads Phantom FG1 XT874 'J' of No 43 Squadron, and Lightning T5s XS417 'Z' and XS419 'T' of 23 Squadron, in late 1974. Until the final days of Nos 5 and 11 Squadrons it was rare for an operational Lightning squadron to have more than a single T-bird on strength. *No 23 Squadron RAF*

ration. The upper pair of nose-mounted Aden guns were deleted from the F3, later considered to be a retrograde step.

XP693, the first of 70 Lightnings completed as F3s (although 10 were converted to later marks) flew on 16 June 1962, and as usual the AFDS was the first RAF user when it accepted XP694 'R' on New Year's Day 1964. Subsequently the F3 formed the major equipment of No 23 Squadron at Leuchars, (August 1964) and Nos 111 and 56 Squadrons at Wattisham (December 1964 and February 1965, respectively) each of which emblazoned their super new fighters with the most eye-catching markings ever seen on postwar RAF fighters. However, 56's red and white chequerboard fins attracted the displeasure of persons in high places, and by the end of 1965 such exotic decor was banned, and markings were toned down to subdued uniformity. April 1967 saw No 56 Squadron posted to Akrotiri permanently to provide air defence for Cyprus, its place being taken at Wattisham by No 29 Squadron which re-formed on 1 May with F3s, mostly made available by the re-equipment of Nos 23 and 74 Squadrons at Leuchars. No 56 Squadron re-equipped in August 1971, No 111 disbanded on 30 September 1974 and No 29 also closed shop as a Lightning unit on the last day of that year — although by then both squadrons had already been re-formed in the air-defence role, equipped with the Phantom FGR2. No 226 OCU also operated F3s, firstly as 145 then as 2T Squadron, and Nos 5 and 11 Squadrons retained about three F3s on strength in addition to their main equipment of F6s. The last

'new' unit to fly F3s was the Lightning Training Flight which shared Binbrook with Nos 5 and 11 Squadrons, and which added several Mk 3s to its inventory early in 1976, and continued to do so until disbandment in April 1987.

A dual-controlled proficiency trainer version of the F3, designated T5, was produced by BAC's Bristol Division at Filton, to maintain employment there. Wg Cdr Jimmy Dell made the first T5 flight, from Filton, on 29 March 1962, XM967 being a conversion from a T4 — as was the second machine, XM966, from which Dell and his observer were obliged to eject on 22 July 1965. They were subsequently safely fished out of the Solway Firth by a Whirlwind helicopter.

A further 22 new-build T5s were produced for the RAF. The second aircraft, XS417, was the first to fly (on 17 July 1964), with XS419 the first to reach an 'operational' unit when, on 20 April 1965 it went to No 226 OCU, the prime user of the mark. A single example also went to each F3 or F6 squadron, and these were often used operationally, even taking their turn on QRA duty. Following the demise of No 226 OCU in September 1974, the T5s formerly flown by that unit's 2T Squadron were mostly transferred to Binbrook where some were stored, a few struck off charge, while several others formed 'C' Flight of No 11

Squadron. This unit temporarily fulfilled the conversion and continuation training role until expanded to establish the Lightning Training Flight in October 1975.

The final new-build version of the Lightning for the RAF stemmed from the eventual realisation by the Air Staff that the aircraft's endurance and range were totally inadequate — not merely for domestic air defence, but more keenly in the matter of overseas reinforcement. Because the Lightning's narrow fuselage was already packed to the gunwales with engines, armament, controls, a pilot, and miles of wiring, the options open to BAC's designers to increase the fuel capacity were somewhat limited. The fifth production F3, XP697, was selected to be rebuilt as the prototype for the new long-range version, initially referred to as the F3*, or F3A, but re-designated F6 prior to squadron service. The metamorphosis took more than a year to complete, and when on 17 April 1964 'Bee' Beamont took XP697 on its first airing over Filton, viewers could readily appreciate why! In its new guise the belly tank had been enlarged to massive proportions to contain 600gal of fuel, yet was skilfully area-ruled to create less drag than the original 250gal tank it replaced; this increased average sortie duration to about 1hr 10min and the greater weight called for take-offs with full reheat. The outer sections of the wings were kinked by extending the new-cambered leading edge, and incorporated wide chord tips which reduced drag by 20% and increased range at

A pair of No 23 Squadron F6s take a tow from a No 214 Squadron Victor tanker. They are over the Niagara Falls during their visit to Toronto at the end of August 1968. *MoD*

subsonic cruising speeds. (This modified wing had originally been tested on P1A WG760 years earlier.) BAC's ingenuity went even further, for the F6's main spar was beefed up to enable a streamlined, jettisonable fuel tank to be mounted above each wing; this unique installation was primarily intended to boost the ferry range of the aircraft for overseas redeployments, since the tanks were not stressed for combat manoeuvres.

Sixty-two Lightning F6s were delivered to the RAF, the first, XR752, flying on 16 June 1965, and the last, XS938, on 30 June 1967. Once again the first customer for the new Lightning was the AFDS, when it received XR753 on 16 November 1965, at Binbrook, where it was renamed the Fighter Command Trials Unit on 1 February 1966. Meanwhile No 5 Squadron at the same base had begun to receive F6s with the arrival of XR755 and XR756 on 10 December 1965. All these early Binbrook aircraft were Interim F6s, which lacked the ability to carry over-wing tanks as well as some other minor equipment; they were later 'modded' by the manufacturer. When the FCTU disbanded on 30 June 1966 its four F6s were transferred to No 23 Squadron at Leuchars which gradually re-equipped with a mixture of Interim and full-production F6s, while its companion squadron, No 74, began to receive the later version from August 1966. Toting over-wing tanks, several of 74's F6s set about testing the new mark's endurance capabilities (and those of their pilots!) by orbiting the UK, frequently taking on nourishment from Marham-based Victor tankers; and in January 1967 four of the new F6s flew Leuchars-Akrotiri non-stop, replenished *en route* by the Victors. On 4 June that year No 74's unrivalled long-range experience with Lightnings reached fulfilment in Exercise 'Hydraulic': this was the rapid redeployment of the squadron's entire complement of 13 F6s from Leuchars to their new base, Tengah, on Singapore Island, 9,250 miles away. Led by the CO Wg Cdr Ken Goodwin the squadron was fully operational at Tengah within five days of its departure from Scotland, having staged through Akrotiri, Cyprus, Masirah in the Persian Gulf, and Gan Island in the Indian ocean, supported by Victor tankers.

No 11 Squadron, which had reformed at Leuchars with F6s on 1 April 1967, took over from No 74 Squadron, and the same year saw the introduction of several innovations to the Lightning, notably the addition of a light to the probe, which eased the task of in-flight refuelling at night. In March a spring-loaded arrester hook, fitted beneath the rear fuselage of an F6, had been successfully tested at Leuchars, and led to its subsequent installation on most Mk 2, 2A, 3, 5 and 6 aircraft.

Above:

An F1A cockpit. The scope for the AI23 is top right. The main instruments in the three panels above the stick are, left to right, altimeter (immediately above rate of climb indicator), altitude indicator, and navigation display. *BAe*

Below:

The F6 cockpit differed in several respects from the F1s, including the airspeed strip display instead of the Machmeter 'clock'. The interior was mainly light grey. *BAe*

F2A was the designation applied to the 31 F2s which were converted by BAC to incorporate some of the range improvements of the F6. Basically these modifications comprised fitting the enlarged belly tank, square-cut fin and kinked wing, but the variant was not stressed for over-wing tanks. During 1968/69 Nos 19 and 92 Squadrons gradually exchanged their F2s for F2As, which were well-liked by their pilots; each squadron retained one or two 'plain' F2s, used mainly on TFF duties. From May 1972 onwards the upper surfaces of the Gütersloh-based Lightnings were camouflaged matt Dark Green as part of a general toning-down. By this time many of these aircraft had

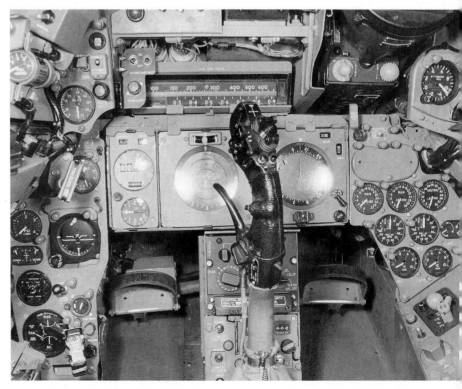

Above:
A Lightning F53, 53-696 '226' of No 2 Squadron with its successor in Royal Saudi AF service, the McDonnell F-15C Eagle.

about 3,000 flying hours to their credit, generally far more than any other Lightnings in service and in part a reflection of their high utilisation and the good serviceability upon which Nos 19 and 92 Squadrons took so much pride. Their age caused most of the F2As to be processed through No 60 MU for re-wiring — a time-consuming task and one which proved to be extremely costly, since within a comparatively short time these same aircraft were destined to be withdrawn from service. Nos 19 and 92 Squadrons disbanded on 1 January and 31 March 1977 respectively, and were replaced by Phantom squadrons which took over their number-plates.

Small detachments of British-based Lightnings were also a frequent sight at RAF Gütersloh in the early 1970s, and some F6s even temporarily operated out of the Luftwaffe base at Fassberg, located close to the East German border, where they practised rapid reaction response. From 1970 the majority of Lightning F6s were modified to carry a pair of 30mm Aden cannon with 120 rounds per gun in the forward compartment of the ventral tank, fuel being retained in the main, rear section. The addition of guns was felt desirable in view of the greatly increased number of interceptions of

Soviet intelligence-gathering aircraft, as it enabled the Lightning pilot to 'warn-off' the Russians should serious confrontation ever occur — whereas the previous total reliance upon the fighter's all-missile armament precluded such an option.

EXPORTS

The belly-tank cannon ports had first been introduced on the export version of the F6, designated F53. Some 34 of these were ordered by Saudi Arabia late in 1965, together with six T55 trainers which differed from the T5 in possessing the enlarged belly tank of the F6 and the extended, cambered, kinked wing — refinements which the RAF could not afford to fit retrospectively to its Mk 5s! This £100 million contract included technical and training support by British civilian companies (including Airwork Ltd) plus the prior delivery of former RAF aircraft comprising two T4s and five F2s (previously mentioned), two Hunter T7s, and pre-production Lightning Mk 1 XG313 used for ground instruction; Royal Saudi Air Force pilots were trained on four T55s at No 226 OCU, Coltishall.

The F53's wing was strengthened to carry 1,000lb of ordnance from a pylon beneath each wingtip, in addition to the over-wing hard points, and a special

photographic reconnaissance pack could be fitted forward of the belly tank. An RAF Lightning F3, XR722, was converted to become the F53 prototype: it first flew as such on 19 October 1966, bearing the 'B' class registration G-27-2 as well as the RSAF number 53-666. Similarly, T5 XS460 became the T55 prototype, flying on 31 January 1966 as 55-710.

The advance delivery of F52s and T54s to Saudi Arabia, codenamed 'Magic Carpet', took place during 1966 to familiarise RSAF air and ground crews and pave the way prior to the main establishment of F53s and T55s. Deliveries of these definitive versions were made by both civilian and serving RAF pilots, during 1968/69, in a programme referred to as 'Magic Palm', and was concluded 12 months later with a few attrition replacement aircraft which brought Middle Eastern Lightning sales to a total of 61. Quite a number of former RAF air and ground crews with Lightning experience served in Saudi Arabia (and Kuwait) to provide a backbone of training and technical support.

In Saudi service the Lightning was used in anger for the only time in its entire career wherein a number of the aircraft used 2in rockets to help rout an intrusion by Yemeni rebels, at that time involved in a threatening border dispute. The aircraft involved were F53s attached to No 6 Squadron operating out of Khamis Mushayt between December 1969 and May 1970, and it was while returning from one of these sorties that 53-697 crashed inside the Yemen on 3 May. The pilot, who ejected safely, was picked up by a rescue C-130 Hercules with Lightning escorts.

The main RSAF Lightning units comprised No 2 Squadron with about 10 F53s at Dhahran in August 1970, later operating from Tabuk: No 13 Squadron operated several F53s; and the Lightning Conversion Unit, also at Dhahran, which flew all six T55s plus about five F53s. Remaining Lightnings were kept by the Lightning Storage Unit at Riyadh, from which attrition replacements were drawn for the relatively high number which were damaged or written off. The last Lightning to be produced was in fact an F53 built from half-completed components, and, as the 339th example of the species, flew on its maiden flight from Warton.

From 1980 onwards F-15 Eagles supplemented then replaced the RSAF Lightnings which were withdrawn from use in December 1985, and on 14 January 1986, 22 surviving aircraft were ferried back to Warton, in three waves, by RAF pilots specially seconded from Binbrook for the operation. Since then the 18 F53s and four T55s have languished in open storage.

Shortly after the Saudi decision to buy Lightnings, Kuwait ordered 12 F53s and two T55s which remained operational for over 10 years before being supplanted by Mirage F1s in 1980/81.

RAF RUN-DOWN

RAF Lightning strength was at a peak in 1968-70 with nine front line operational squadrons plus a large OCU, giving a combined total of about 150 aircraft plus a few reserves — barely enough aeroplanes to sustain this force, after consideration of those undergoing major overhaul, together with others involved in lengthy second-line servicing. The disbandment in August 1971 of No 74 Squadron at RAF Tengah and the 'handing down' of its Lightning F6s to No 56 Squadron in Cyprus, alleviated the shortage to some extent.

The Lightning's intended successor was the McDonnell-Douglas F-4 Phantom, already in service with No 43 Squadron at Leuchars in the FG1 air defence role since 1969. With the release of FGR2 Phantoms formerly employed as tactical fighters, the replacement of short-endurance, missile-only armed Lightning F3s took place in the last half of 1974 when Nos 111 and 29 Squadrons were re-equipped with the two-seat American fighter. The F-4 superseded the Lightning F6 with No 23 Squadron in October 1975, with 56 Squadron by the summer of 1976, and continuing to assume its dominance by replacing the two German-based Lightning squadrons by April 1977.

Shortly after this came the (slow) realisation that RAF air defence interceptor assets were minimal and without adequate reserves, and while the Lightning was seen as yesterday's fighter in terms of radar, armament and endurance, its performance was still on a par with the best. There being over 80 available — of which barely 30 F3s and F6s were in regular front-line service with the two operational squadrons — the government therefore announced in July 1979 its decision to re-establish a third operational squadron at Binbrook as a short-term measure pending the availability of the Tornado ADV in the mid-1980s. Although No 45 was the squadron number unofficially publicised as the unit's intended identity, the new squadron would have been No 74 — but after months of procrastination it was axed before it could even take wing, after the Treasury yet again became an obstacle and also it became apparent that there were insufficient younger pilots.

However, the LTF had started to train more first-tourist fast jet pilots by then, and one of the results was the creation, in late 1981, of the Lightning Augmentation Force (LAF) which acted as a refresher flying unit for former Lightning pilots, thereby creating a war reserve; it had no aircraft of its own but was able to draw upon those rotated between storage and the squadrons,

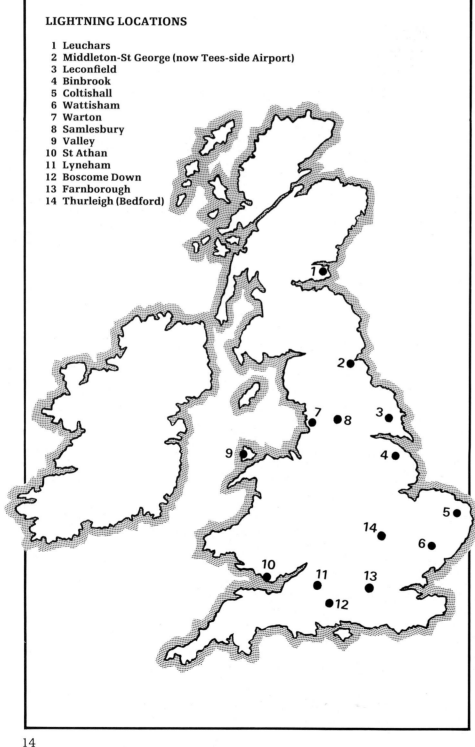

LIGHTNING LOCATIONS

1 Leuchars
2 Middleton-St George (now Tees-side Airport)
3 Leconfield
4 Binbrook
5 Coltishall
6 Wattisham
7 Warton
8 Samlesbury
9 Valley
10 St Athan
11 Lyneham
12 Boscome Down
13 Farnborough
14 Thurleigh (Bedford)

some of which carried a small 'LAF' logo self-adhesive fluorescent red sticker on the fin.

Slippage of the Tornado ADV's service entry date brought yet another reprieve for the Lightning, and after tests on British Aerospace's F6 XP697, funds were released for a refurbishment programme in 1985 which involved the strengthening of the wing roots on about 30 F6s; referred to as Mod 9, the work was carried out at Binbrook by a British Aerospace engineering team assisted by the RAF, and it extended the fatigue life of the airframe by a further 400 flying hours.

For some years the Lightning force had been subjected to regular detailed engineering checks, including X-ray inspections, to ensure the physical integrity of the airframe and systems components, with fatigue meter readings monitoring induced stress after every flight; similarly aircraft have been rotated regularly between active squadron service and spells in storage, to distribute fatigue. Because it had never been envisaged that the Lightning would remain in service for so long, inadequate spares provisioning became a problem in the 1980s — only solved by the ingenuity of Binbrook's Engineering Wing. The disbandment of the LTF in April 1987 and the demise of No 5 Squadron from November that year resulted in salvaged components becoming available to help keep No 11 Squadron's Lightnings flying, although the cessation of overhauls by Rolls-Royce of the aircraft's Avon engines still posed difficulties. In December 1987 three or four Lightnings were assigned to a special programme linked with Tornado F3 development. Recently-posted engineering staff were recalled to Binbrook to help prepare these Lightnings for a further spell of service, possibly beyond the expiry date of No 11 Squadron. These Lightnings were flown with over-wing tanks, and in this context it is pertinent to recall that for several years previously, Lightnings in this same configuration have been operated by the squadrons to simulate Soviet 'Backfire' and 'Blinder' bombers, because of their similar radar signature. The Lightning has also been considered for use as a pilotless target drone, though in the event this rôle never materialised.

Above:
Lightning F53 53-417, destined for Kuwait. *BAe*

Below:
Weathered and worn out! XR727 'BH' goes round the Binbrook circuit during Exercise 'Mallet Blow' on 17 March 1988. It is in typical condition for the last months of No 11s Lightnings. *John Dunnell*

15

Above:
F1 XM144, the 'Queen of the Sky' and pride and joy of Wattisham TFF, with undercarriage just lowering to land at Benson in September 1970. Also shown are the original straight leading edge wing, 250gal ventral tank and Firestreak missiles.
Brian Lowe

Below:
By comparison with XM144, F6 XR747 'K' of No 23 Squadron (on finals to Upper Heyford on 28 August 1970) shows the changes which had been incorporated in this last RAF variant: a kinked/cambered leading edge wing of greater area, a much enlarged 600gal ventral tank (at this time lacking the two 30mm cannon armament, flight refuelling probe, Red Top missiles and arrester hook. *Brian Lowe*

Lightning Data

LIGHTNING VARIANTS COMPARISON

Variant	Engines	Weights	Dimensions	Principal distinguishing features
P1A	2 × Armstrong-Siddeley Saphire 5, 7,500lb each; later replaced by Saphire 5R 9,200lb with reheat	22,221lb empty; 27,077lb loaded	Span: 34ft 10in; Length: 49ft 8in; Height: 17ft 3in; Wing area: 458.5sq ft	Original prototypes to F23/49. Max speed Mach 1.53 (1,011mph) at 36,000ft
P1B	2 × Rolls-Royce Avon 200R (later 210R) 14,430lb each with reheat	24,816lb empty; 31,831lb loaded; 34,140lb max loaded	Span: 34ft 10in; Length: 55ft 3in; Height: 19ft 5in; Wing area: 458.5sq ft	Fighter prototypes. Max speed Mach 2.1 (1,390mph) at 40,000ft
Lightning F1	2 × Rolls-Royce Avon 200R	25,753lb empty	As P1B except height: 19ft 7in	First production version, AI23 radar, VHF radio (later replaced by UHF), 2 × 30mm Aden cannon in nose and 2 Firestreak missiles (or alternative weapons pack). Mach 2.2 approx
Lightning F1A	2 × Rolls-Royce Avon 210R with revised, four-position reheat throttle control	25,737lb empty	As F1	First version with in-flight refuelling capability (detachable probe, fitment beneath port wing), UHF radio, external cable ducts to missile pylon positions
Lightning F2	2 × Rolls-Royce Avon 210R with fully variable reheat control	27,000lb (approx) empty	As F1	Revised cockpit including partial OR946 specification, liquid oxygen breathing system, standby turbo generator for DC electric supply (identified by small cooling scoop on dorsal spine)
Lightning F2A	2 × Rolls-Royce Avon 211R	27,500lb (approx) empty	As F1 except wing area: 474.5sq ft	F2 rebuilt to incorporate some F6 features: kinked, cambered wing; square-cut fin; enlarged ventral fuel tank. Retained 2 × 30mm Aden cannon in upper nose. Firestreak missiles
Lightning F3	2 × Rolls-Royce Avon 301R, 12,690lb thrust (dry) and 16,360lb thrust (reheat)	26,905lb empty	As F1	Square-cut fin of 15% greater area, deletion of built-in cannon armament, more advanced AI23B radar which allowed equipment with either Red Top collision-course missiles or Firestreak. Full OR946 Integrated Flight System instrumentation
Lightning F3A (Interim F6)	2 × Rolls-Royce Avon 301R	28,041lb empty; 41,700lb loaded	As F3 except wing area: 474.5sq ft	Kinked, cambered wing of greater area, and enlarged ventral fuel tank

Variant	Engines	Weights	Dimensions	Principal distinguishing features
Lightning T4	2 × Rolls-Royce Avon 210R	27,000lb (approx) empty	As F1	Two-seat, dual-controlled trainer version of F1A; deletion of cannon from upper nose
Lightning T5	2 × Rolls-Royce Avon 301R	27,000lb (approx) empty	As F3	Two-seat, dual-controlled trainer version of F3, with capability of carrying either Firestreak or Red Top missiles
Lightning F6	2 × Rolls-Royce Avon 301R	28,041lb empty; 41,700lb max loaded	As F3A	Full production version of F3A with provision to carry over-wing fuel tanks, and some small improvements to equipment
Lightning F53	2 × Rolls-Royce Avon 302C	Similar to F6	As F3A	Export version of F6 with capability to carry wide range of ordnance from over-wing or under-wing pylon hard-points. AI23S radar (export version of AI23B)
Lightning T55	2 × Rolls-Royce Avon 302C	Similar to F6	As F3A	Export version of T5, with enlarged ventral fuel tank; kinked, cambered wing and AI23S

Modifications

In the course of its long RAF service most versions of the Lightning were subject to the incorporation of many modifications, mostly without significant external evidence of change. Many were concerned with improving the fire prevention integrity of the engine bays and jet pipes, where the incidence of fires caused the loss of a high proportion of the Lightnings which were written off in flying accidents. Modifications to operational equipment were relatively few because they were not considered cost effective in an aircraft which was not expected to remain in service for more than a decade! However, limited improvements were made to the AI23B radar, resulting in AI23C and finally AI23D versions.

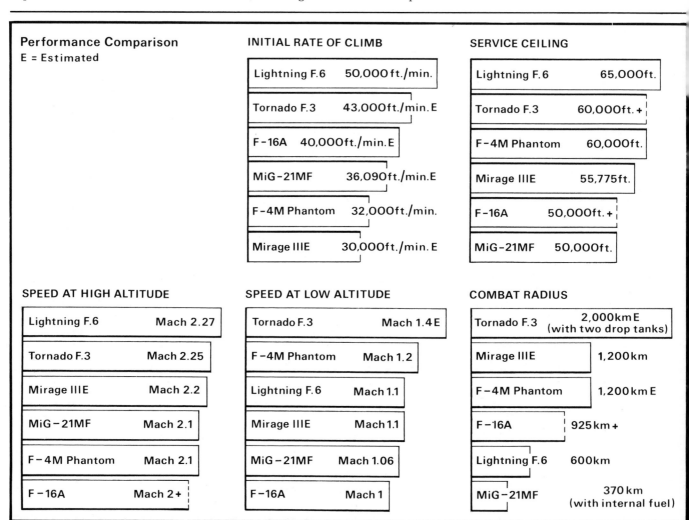

Performance Comparison
E = Estimated

INITIAL RATE OF CLIMB

Lightning F.6	50,000 ft./min.
Tornado F.3	43,000 ft./min. E
F-16A	40,000 ft./min. E
MiG-21MF	36,090 ft./min. E
F-4M Phantom	32,000 ft./min.
Mirage IIIE	30,000 ft./min. E

SERVICE CEILING

Lightning F.6	65,000 ft.
Tornado F.3	60,000 ft. +
F-4M Phantom	60,000 ft.
Mirage IIIE	55,775 ft.
F-16A	50,000 ft. +
MiG-21MF	50,000 ft.

SPEED AT HIGH ALTITUDE

Lightning F.6	Mach 2.27
Tornado F.3	Mach 2.25
Mirage IIIE	Mach 2.2
MiG-21MF	Mach 2.1
F-4M Phantom	Mach 2.1
F-16A	Mach 2 +

SPEED AT LOW ALTITUDE

Tornado F.3	Mach 1.4 E
F-4M Phantom	Mach 1.2
Lightning F.6	Mach 1.1
Mirage IIIE	Mach 1.1
MiG-21MF	Mach 1.06
F-16A	Mach 1

COMBAT RADIUS

Tornado F.3	2,000 km E (with two drop tanks)
Mirage IIIE	1,200 km
F-4M Phantom	1,200 km E
F-16A	925 km +
Lightning F.6	600 km
MiG-21MF	370 km (with internal fuel)

LIGHTNING PRODUCTION DETAILS

Variant	Number built and flown	Serials	Construction numbers
P1A	2	WG760, 763	95001, 95003
P1B Prototype	3	XA847, 853, 856	95004-006
Development batch	20	XG307-313, 325-337	95007-026
Lightning F1	19	XM134-147, 163-167	95030-048
Lightning F1A	28	XM169-192, 213-216	95056-070, 082-095
Lighting F2	44	XN723-735, 767-797	95096, 094, 097-099, 105-110, 113-115, 121-150
Lightning F3	70	XP693-708, 735-765, XR711-728, 747-751	95116-120, 151-193, 95194-216
Lighting F3A (interim F6)	16	XR752-767	95217-232
P11	2	XL628, 629 (T4 prototypes)	95049, 050
Lightning T4	20	XM966-974, 987-997	95051-055, 071-080, 100, 101, 104, 103, 111 respectively
Lightning T5	22	XS416-423, 449-460, XV328, 329	B1/95001-B1/95022
Lightning F6	38	XR768-773, XS893-904, 918-938	95233-238, 95239-271
Lightning F53	46	53-667 to 53-700 (RSAF); 412-423 (Kuwait)	95272-291, 293-298, 300, 306, 317 respectively (RSAF); 95292, 299, 307-316 (Kuwait)
Lightning T55	8	55-711 to 55-716 (RSAF); 410, 411 (Kuwait)	B1/95024-028, 030 (RSAF); B1/95023, 029 (Kuwait)
	338 in total		

CANCELLATIONS

Lightning F1	3	XM148, 149, 168
Lightning F1A	2	XM217, 218
Lightning F2	11	XN798-808
Lightning F3	22	XR774-795
Lightning T4	10	XN103-112
Lightning T5	5	XS851-855
Lightning F6	12	

STATIC TEST AIRFRAMES

	Quantity	Serial allocation	Construction number
P1A	1	WG765	95002
Lightning F1	3	XM131-133	95027-029

CONVERSIONS

	Quantity	Serials
P1B (DB) to F3	1	XG310 (to serve as prototype)
F2 to F2A	31	XN724, 726-728, 730-733, 735, 771-778, 780-784, 786-793, 795
F2 to F3	1	XN725
F2 to F3A	1	XN734
F2 to F52	5	XN729, 767, 770, 796, 797 respectively becoming 52-659, 655, 656, 657, 658 in RSAF service. (In 1967 the survivors were re-serialled: 659=612; 655=609; 656=610; 658=611.)
T4 to T5	2	XM966, 967
F3 to F6	9	XP693, 697, XR723-728, 747
F3 to F53	1	XR722 becoming 53-666 in RSAF service
F3A to F6	16	XR752-767
T4 to T54	2	XM989, 992 becoming 54-650 and 651 (re-serialled as 64-607 and 64-608 in 1967)
T5 to T55	1	XS460 becoming 55-710 with RSAF

LENGTH OF OPERATIONAL/REGULAR SERVICE

RAF Lightning units	1959	60	61	62	63	64	65	66	67	68	69	70	71	72	73	74	75	76	77	78	79	80	81	82	83	84	85	86	87	88
5 Sqn							11/65 interim F6		4/67 full standard F6																				11/87	
11 Sqn									4/67					9/74 'C' Flt 10/75 T5															- 4/88	
19 Sqn				12/62 F2						4/68 Gradual intro of F2A								12/76												
23 Sqn						8/64 F3				5/68 F6						10/75														
29 Sqn									5/67 F3						12/74															
56 Sqn			12/60 F1A				1/65 F3						8/71 F6				6/75													
74 Sqn		6/60 F1				4/64 F3		8/66 F6					8/71																	
92 Sqn				3/63 F2						6/68 F2A									3/77											
111 Sqn			3/61 F1A			11/64 F3										9/74														
AFDS/ FCTU	12/59 F1			10/62 F2 1/64 F3			11/65 F6	6/67																						
LCS/ 226 OCU				6/62 T4 6/63 F1 6/64 F1A 4/65 T5								6/70 F3				9/74														
LTF																	10/75 T5, F3		+ F6										4/87	
TTF								2/66 F1 F1A							12/73															
Approx Number of RAF Lightnings in service		12/60 18	12/61 42	12/62 50	12/63 80	12/64 94	12/65 96	12/66 125	12/67 146	12/68 150	12/69 150	12/70 150	12/71 135	12/72 135	12/73 126	12/74 82	12/75 58	12/76 45	12/77 35	→									5/87 28	12/87 18	6/88 NIL
Number of RAF Lightnings written off (Cat 5)	3	1	1	3	5	3	5	6	5	1	7	10	5	2	3	2	1	1	—	3	—	1	—	1	1	1	1	1	1	Total: 1 74
Approximate accident rate as % of aircraft in RAF service	16·7	2·4	2·0	3·7	5·3	3·2	4·0	4·1	3·4	0·6	4·7	7·4	3·7	1·6	3·6	3·4	2·3	2·8	—	8·5	—	2·8	—	2·8	2·8	2·8	2·8	2·8	6·2	

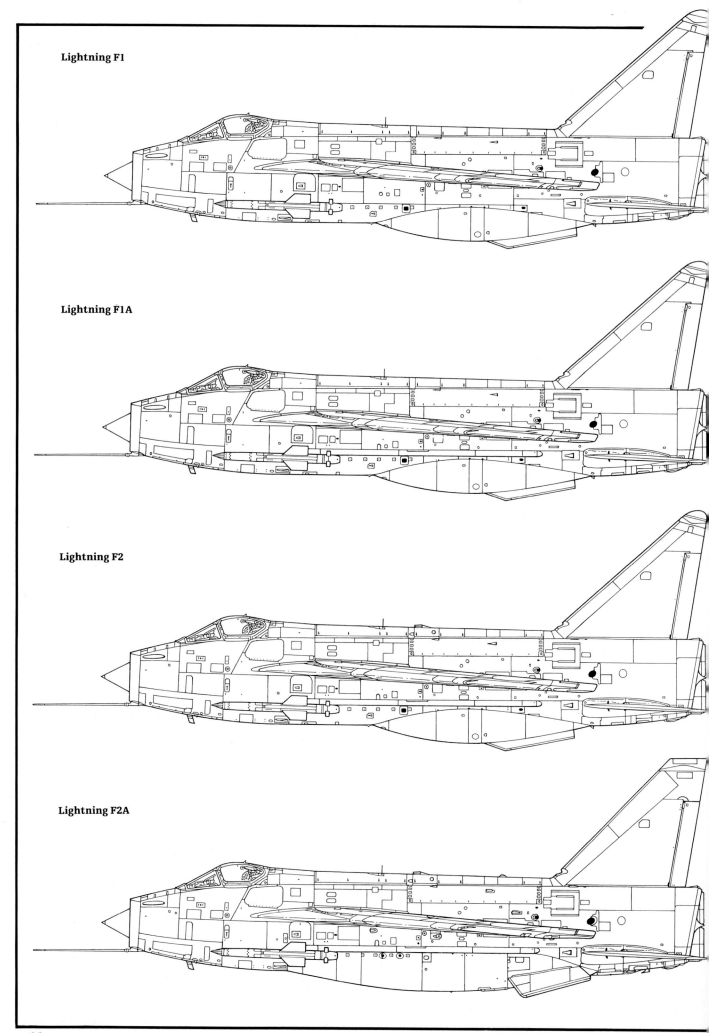

Lightning F1

Lightning F1A

Lightning F2

Lightning F2A

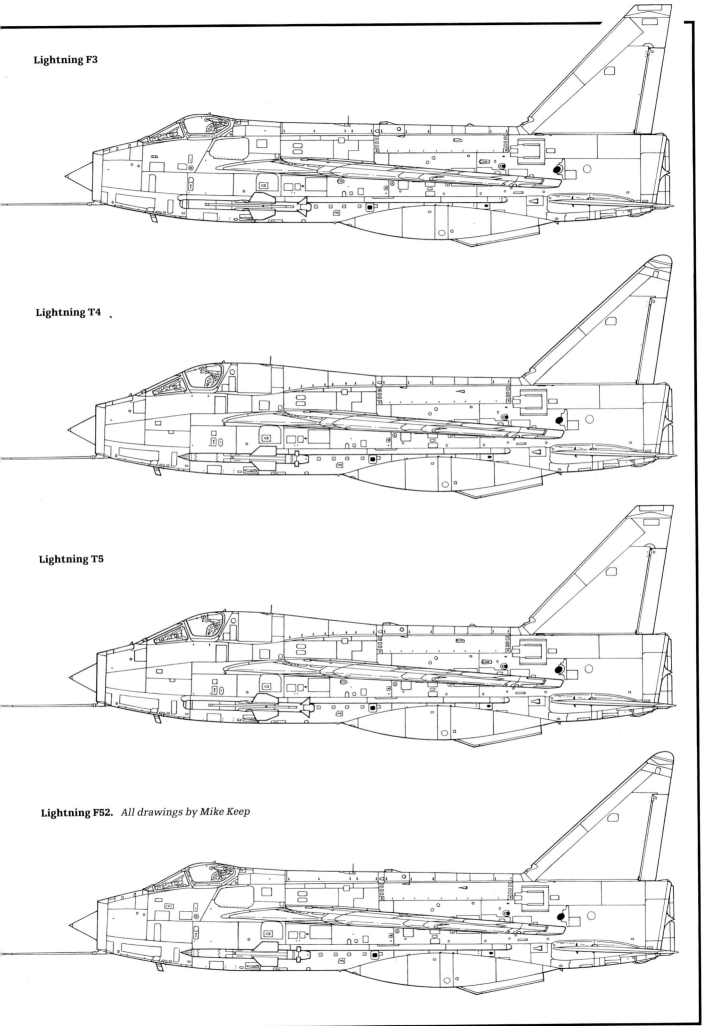

Lightning F3

Lightning T4

Lightning T5

Lightning F52. *All drawings by Mike Keep*

Lightning Flying

Sqn Ldr Tony Paxton has flown every mark of Lightning in RAF service, flying the aircraft with No 226 OCU, Nos 5, 11 and 19 Squadrons and the LTF. He then did two operational tours on 'bombers', flying Tornado GR1s with Nos 9 and 31 Squadrons before returning to the air defence role via a conversion course on No 229 OCU. This was a prelude to joining No 5 Squadron at Coningsby flying the latest Tornado F3s, where he was one of the unit's most experienced pilots and is now a Flight Commander with No 23 Squadron flying Tornado F3s from Leeming. Apart from initial pilot training all of his flying career has been within the 'fast jet fraternity', where he has notched up well over 2,000 hours on Lightnings and more than 1,200 on Tornados.

Tony is an accomplished photographer and his superb air-to-air studies have been published in several books and magazines including *Aircraft Illustrated*. His 'Lightning Flying' contribution also shows his considerable ability as a writer.

———

'At RAF Leeming during the summer of 1969 I was learning to fly the Jet Provost with 3 FTS; the last aircraft that I wanted to fly on completion of my training was the Lightning!

'The staff at the flying training schools can influence their students with enthusiasm, or lack of it, for their old role or aircraft. When I went through Leeming there were no ex-Lightning pilots on the staff. Also the Harrier and Phantom were just about to enter service so mud-moving was the popular goal. As students our view of the Lightning then was a steep climb to 40,000ft, fly around for twenty minutes with one's head buried in a radar scope, rapid descent and land from a GCA; where was the fun in that? I was to find out!

'By the time that I had done most of my Gnat course at Valley I had decided quite definitely that my overriding wish was to fly single-seat and at the time that meant Harrier or Lightning. There were seven of us on my course and only two fast jet postings; I came second on the course and was posted to Lightnings.

'The Lightning OCU was No 226 at RAF Coltishall in Norfolk and like any other OCU started with four weeks or so of groundschool. However, to whet the students' appetite, day one of the course included a trip in the famous

"aluminium tube"; it was not an instructional sortie, just a marvellous incentive to get down to work in the groundschool.

'Flying the Lightning is a pleasure which every pilot who has had the good fortune to do will always savour, but I was soon to learn that flying the aircraft was something that had to become second nature very quickly. The Lightning is, essentially, a very easy aeroplane to fly; where many pilots have failed is in not having the spare capacity to fly the aircraft and operate its weapon system effectively. The radar hand controller had 14 separate controls all to be operated by the left hand while the pilot interpreted the radar scope, responded to GCI instructions and flew the aircraft accurately on heading, height and speed.

'So, was I spending my days rushing around at 40,000ft? Far from it: during the Coltishall course we covered a lot of low-level exercises, one of which I remember was particularly exciting. The Lightning was designed as a high level interceptor and so the guns were mounted to point slightly upward so that the aircraft could be flown behind

Below:
XN771 'P', the No 19 Squadron Lightning F2A 'assigned' to Tony Paxton when he flew with the squadron in the early 1970s. The fin code is in yellow. *Martin Horseman*

and below the target clear of its slipstream. Imagine a target flying at 50ft; a normal gun firing position would result in the Lightning flying into the sea or ground. So, to achieve a low-level guns kill the following manoeuvre was taught at Coltishall. We flew slightly to one side of the target's track with overtake and about 1,000ft high; as the target started to disappear from view behind the fuselage we rolled inverted, located the target and pulled the nose down through it, rolled upright and the gunsight would be pointing behind the target which was at a range of about 600-700 yards, the Lightning was by now in a fairly steep dive at about 500ft and accelerating. We started firing the guns and pulled the sight up through the target hoping to get some hits; then increased the pull to avoid flying into the sea or ground. This may seem rather haphazard but every round from an Aden 30mm cannon is effectively a hand grenade, meaning that just one hit on a wet wing could bring the target down. It was obvious that life on a Lightning squadron was going to be very different from my original idea at Leeming.

'I arrived at RAF Gütersloh in West Germany on 28 October 1972, exactly four years after I had joined the Air Force. I was posted to No 19 Squadron and about to start three years of the most enjoyable flying I have ever done.

'The Gütersloh wing was equipped with the Lightning F Mk 2A which I would say was the best Lightning ever built. The F2A was an extensively rebuilt version of the F2; externally it resembled the F6 with the large ventral tank, enlarged square-topped fin and extended, cambered leading edge to the wing. Why was it the best? The Rolls-Royce 211 series Avon engines, although less powerful than the 302 series of the F6, were somehow better matched to the airframe and intake. The harmony between engines and airframe gave a very economical performance and required fewer ancillary intakes and projections along the fuselage which made the F2A more slippery than the later mark. On a medium to high level practice interception (PI) sortie it was not uncommon to fly for 1hr 40min, which is not dissimilar to the sorties we are now flying in the Tornado F Mk 3.

'The F2A retained the top guns of the early marks with the option of replacing the Firestreak missile pack with a further pair of Adens. Firing the guns was quite an exiting event. They were mounted 2-3ft behind the pilot with the barrels one each side of the cockpit at about thigh level; when they were fired all hell broke loose in the cockpit. Bulbs would fall out, dust flew around, everything was shaken and there was a strong smell of cordite. Quite often the main flight instruments would fail. This was because the shaking and rattling of the guns firing

Above:
Camouflaged F6 XS928 'L' was photographed by Lightning pilot Sqn Ldr Tony Paxton in March 1978.

could cause the push-pull switch for the master reference gyro to vibrate to the pull/off position; no problem if you realised what had happened but most disconcerting the first time it was experienced.

'There I was on my first Lightning Squadron tour; were my fears from Leeming to be realised? Certainly not; the flying was quite superb and after the six months of training, to become fit to hold Battle Flight (Germany QRA) can only be described as licensed hooliganism. Most of our radar work of PIs was flown on the night shift. The day flying was largely low-level CAP (Combat Air Patrol) or ACT (Air Combat Training). The rules for engaging other aircraft in Germany were simple and flexible. If one encountered another fast jet at low level you could "have a go"; if he reacted the game was on, if he waggled you off he was left alone.

'The Lightning's navigation kit was not marvellous, designed to use radio and tacan beacons which were not available at low level; our radar was next to useless at low level over the land so we were effectively a supersonic Spitfire. If we had to chase a target at low level there was no chance to look at a map so the navigation technique was quite simple. As you left CAP you started the stopwatch and noted the heading; once the kill had been achieved, turn on to the reciprocal heading and fly back for the same time as you had been chasing. Once in the general vicinity of the CAP you were bound to recognise some ground feature or other.

'In 1975 I was posted to No 5 Squadron at RAF Binbrook in Lincolnshire. Flying in the UK was different but still nowhere near my fears from Leeming. No 5 Squadron was equipped with Lightning F MK 6 and F Mk 3s, the only difference between the two being the large ventral tank and cambered leading edge of the F6. These

marks carried an improved radar and front hemisphere Red Top missiles, giving an increased capability over the F2A.

'The Lightning's job in the UK was similar to Germany but the environment was very different. We still flew a lot of low level but it was mostly over the sea and quite a bit of it was at night. The radar performance at low level was reasonable over the sea and with GCI control many successful intercepts were carried out. During these low-level PIs at night the workload became really high particularly if the task was to identify the target visually. The Visident procedure required continual monitoring of the radar scope whilst flying level and accurately on heading which had to be adjusted by 2° or 3° at a time along with very small speed adjustments to position the aircraft for the best chance of visually acquiring the target. A short lapse in concentration could quickly lead to a descent and acceleration towards the sea. We had no radar altimeter and therefore no low height warning. The pressure altimeter suffered from large pressure errors such that at Mach 0.9 the altimeter under-read by 700ft; it was very disconcerting to fly along with the altimeter reading less than zero!

'Navigation in the UK Lightning force was not a major problem; we were generally under GCI control when not overland, and even if not, a quick sweep of the coast on radar was sufficient to determine one's position.

'The UK Lightnings had a head-on capability with their Red Top missiles and setting up the correct geometry for the firing could be quite tricky. The final stages could be exciting too because at missile launch the fighter and target aircraft were on a collision course with a closing speed of around 30 miles a minute. The breakaway manoeuvre was a rapid roll to inverted and pull to avoid the debris after missile impact.

'I had a marvellous time flying the Lightning; sadly I shall probably never fly it again. The F Mk 2A was certainly my favourite and that has gone for ever anyway.'

RAF Lightning Units & Markings

NO 5 SQUADRON

Formed on 26 July 1913 at Farnborough, it was not until early in 1941 that No 5 became a fighter squadron.

No 5 Squadron re-formed at Binbrook on 8 October 1965 and became the first operational RAF squadron with the F6, although its sole aircraft for the first 10 days was WV318, a Hunter T7A. This was one of eight such aircraft specially modified with OR946 instrumentation for use at Binbrook, Leuchars and Wattisham, pending availability of the Lightning T5 — which in No 5's case was XS451 'T' delivered on 19 November. The squadron had to wait until 10 December for its first single-seaters, XR755 'A', and XR756 'B', which were of the Interim variety. From early 1967 these were replaced by full production standard F6s, and the squadron wasted no time in exploiting the long range capabilities of the aircraft when fitted with over-wing tanks. After gaining experience with 'round Britain' training sorties of up to 7hr duration, being regularly topped up by Victor tankers, No 5 went on to achieve some epic long-range deployments — to the Mediterranean — then on to Bahrain, a distance of 4,000 miles in 8hr. In December 1969 10 of their dozen F6s flew to Tengah in Singapore for joint air defence exercises with the Royal Australian Air force and RAF units in the Far East; although this was not nonstop, it was nevertheless gruelling — the Lightning's cockpit is small, cramped, and hardly the most comfortable situation to spend hours trussed up in immersion suit, life jacket and flying suit! Next year No 5 was back in Singapore, delivering new Lightnings to No 74 Squadron and ferrying others back to Britain for overhaul.

In 1968 and 1969 the 'Fighting Fifth' won the Dacre Trophy for the top UK fighter squadron in weapons proficiency, subsequently repeating this success; in May 1970 it added to its collection the Huddleston Trophy, awarded to the best NATO interceptor squadron. Early in 1971 the two Lightning F1As of the Binbrook Target Facilities Flight were absorbed into

Above:
F6 XS922 'H' approaches Luqa, Malta circa 1969, still without the ventral gun pack.
Dennis Robinson

No 5 Squadron, which in addition to continuing in the same role used them for several solo aerobatic displays, as they were lighter and more nimble than the F6s. The F1As left the squadron, but not the base when the Binbrook TFF was reformed in September 1972, and the next month No 5 was issued with several F3s.

In common with No 11 Squadron, destined to share Binbrook for the next 15 years, two or three of the unit's F3s were retained for target facilities purposes and aerobatics. The distinction of providing the solo aero display went to No 5 Squadron in its final year with the Lightning, at the conclusion of the show 'season' in September 1987, after which the F3s were promptly scrapped! Earlier that month the squadron participated in its final Missile Practice Camp at Valley, when more generous quotas of Firestreaks and Red Tops were launched than hitherto, since these weapons would be redundant after the imminent withdrawal of the Lightning from front-line service.

Saturday 7 November 1987 saw No 5 Squadron host a reunion and put up a

final nine-ship formation for the benefit of Geoffrey Lee, a British Aerospace photographer flying in a Hawk from Chivenor. Thereafter the run down was quite swift, with most pilots being posted away, although a few moved over to No 11 Squadron. The last Lightning sorties were flown a few days before Christmas, closing a unique chapter in the squadron's history and ending its 22-year association with the same type of aircraft operated from the same airfield — a record which is unlikely to be broken.

Markings

Red rectangles each side of the nose roundel characterised the unit's markings for much of its time with Lightnings. Fin markings initially comprised a small white disc, with a two-tone green and black maple leaf superimposed; the individual aircraft letter was in black near the fin tip.

In 1970 the white fin disc was encircled by a large red '5'.

With the introduction of matt Dark Green and Dark Sea Grey camouflage to the upper surfaces of Binbrook's Light-

Above:
F6 XS923 'C', with revised fin markings and fitted with ventral gun pack, shimmers in autumnal sunshine at Binbrook. The liquid on the tarmac is a mix of spilt kerosene and water used to disperse it. *Author*

Below:
No 5 Squadron's F6 XR726 'K', still adorned with No 23 Squadron markings following the 25th anniversary celebrations, lost its rudder on 15 August 1979 on return from Sola, Norway. *Robin Walker*

nings from the autumn of 1975, the nose markings were reduced in size and by early 1977 code letters were changed to white.

The following year experimental markings were briefly applied to two F6s; XR770 'B' reverted to a black code letter with a small green maple leaf above the fin flash; while XS898 'J' wore a red horizontal stripe across the fin, on which a green maple leaf was centred, with the code letter beneath it in red. both schemes were intended to make the aircraft even less conspicuous when flying low-level overland.

Towards the latter part of 1980 the Binbrook Lightning units adopted double letter codes, 'A' being allocated to No 5, 'B' to No 11, 'C' to the planned third squadron (which never materialised), and 'D' to the LTF.

The CO's aircraft, XR770 'AA', was the first operational Lightning F6 to introduce the new semi-matt 'Barley Grey' paint scheme, in the summer of 1981, and was unique in initially having full-size roundels adopted with this 'air superiority' decor. Squadron markings, consisting of a green maple leaf flanked by small red bars, were applied to the fin, and code letters were white. Thereafter about 60% of the Binbrook Lightnings received some

Top:
T5 XV328 'T' of No 5 Squadron. *Tony Paxton*

Above:
XS935 'AK' is adorned in the special markings applied in October 1986 to celebrate No 5 Squadron's 21 years with Lightnings. *Peter Cooper*

form of grey treatment, but there were several variations of it, as progressively darker shades and lower demarcation lines were adopted. Squadron markings were standardised on the fin, with the maple leaf set against a pale blue disc.

While the squadron was deployed on its annual Armament Practice Camp visit to Akrotiri, Cyprus, for live gunnery practice during the summer of

1984, three of its F6s acquired sharksteeth markings, which were retained for several weeks after their return to the UK. The aircraft involved were once again XR770 'AA', plus XR754 'AE' and XS903 'AM'.

In October 1986 the squadron celebrated its 70th anniversary by flying a diamond-nine formation and painting several of its F6s with special markings: XS935 'AK' and XS899 'AM'

re-introduced the '5' on the fin and red bars adjacent to the nose roundels, while XS897 'AC', a grey and green camouflaged machine, reverted to full size 'D' roundels and markings representative of No 5's earliest Lightning days. Pride of place went to XR770 'AA', the aircraft assigned to the CO, Wg Cdr 'Andy' Williams, which had the fin painted scarlet. In some instances these markings were retained until the squadron disposed of its Lightnings, but in the closing months of its No 5 service, red was extended to the fuselage spine and leading edges of the wings of XR770, bringing a colourful conclusion to the longest serving Lightning squadron.

NO 11 SQUADRON

The squadron's existence dates from 14 February 1915 when it formed at Netheravon, Wiltshire with Vickers FB.5 two-seat scout biplanes. Re-formed at Leuchars on 1 April 1967 with some of the final factory-fresh Lightning F6s, No 11 was the replacement squadron for No 74 which departed to Singapore in June that year. No 11 shared with similarly equipped No 23 Squadron the policing of Britain's most northerly air defence zone, which extends to beyond the Shetlands and includes the Faroes Gap. It is this area which receives most intrusions from long-range Soviet reconnaissance aircraft, at times considerably more than one a day. No 11 achieved its fair share of scrambles from the 'Q' sheds at Leuchars, to intercept these Soviet 'Zombies' by day and by night, 365 days a year. Invariably supported by Victor tankers, to enable the fighters to remain airborne to shepherd the 'Bears', 'Bisons', 'Badgers' or Soviet maritime reconnaissance planes away from British shores, the Lightnings often used to recover to Lossiemouth or other airfields north of Leuchars if fuel was running low.

In common with other F6 squadrons, No 11 took part in several long-range redeployment exercises, and on 6 January 1969 10 F6s left Leuchars for Singapore, 9,180 miles and 18½ flying hours away, staging via Muharraq in the Persian Gulf and the island of Gan in the Indian Ocean. By the time they had returned home to Scotland a total of 228 flight refuelling contacts with Victor tankers had been notched up. Other notable events included Exercise 'Lime Jug 70' in Malta in October 1970;

and participation by two aircraft in the Paris Air Show in May 1971 had XR757 'D' continuing to sport its show identification number for many months after the event, with '469' painted amidships in large black numerals.

From September 1969, when No 43 re-formed at Leuchars with Phantom FG1s, increasing reliance had been placed on these much longer-ranged and more heavily armed two-seaters. As the Leuchars' Phantom force was gradually expanded, so the Lightnings were displaced, beginning with No 11 which moved south on 22 March 1972 to take up residence at Binbrook, joining No 5 Squadron, a partnership which was to endure more than 16 years.

Thereafter No 11's history parallels that of No 5 Squadron, with the exception of its temporary enlargement in the autumn of 1974 by 'C' Flight to take over the task of training new Lightning pilots and providing refresher flying for others, following the closure of No 226 OCU at Coltishall in September. Operating four or five T5s, 'C' Flight was hived off to form the Lightning Training Flight in October 1975.

Together with No 5, No 11 contributed aircraft for the Lightning's 25th anniversary celebrations at Binbrook in August 1979, when a spectacular Lightning flying display was planned. This was to include solo aerobatics, a four-ship formation aerobatics team provided by No 5 Squadron and a fly-past of nine Lightnings each adorned in the different markings of one of the nine squadrons which had been equipped with the type. The climax was intended to be a massed formation of 25 Lightnings, and as a prelude to this, practice flights took place in late July, beginning with a 10-ship formation on the 20th, then 17 aircraft on the 27th, building up to 24 on 31 July.

Unfortunately, the day chosen for the celebrations, Friday 3rd, provided typical British summer weather, and although the singleton and four-ship team put on a brave show in appalling conditions, the larger formations had to be cancelled. However, nothing could diminish the indoor conviviality, as Binbrook hosted more then 200 former Lightning pilots and many distinguished guests including Sir Frederick Page and Roland Beamont.

The weather was much the same for the 'Last Last Lightning Show' in August 1987 though on this occasion it failed to prevent 11 Lightnings from becoming airborne, including a strong contingent from No 11 Squadron which was destined to become the last operational squadron. No 11 strength actually increased to 16 Lightning F6s plus a T5 at the beginning of 1988, when it had 15 pilots, including a few transferred from No 5 Squadron. At this time several aircraft were fitted with over-wing tanks for some special long-endurance flights in conjunction with a British Aerospace Tornado F3 trials programme. Despite the knowledge that the unit would soon be stood down, No 11 maintained its full operational commitment throughout the early spring, including MPC at Valley, live gunnery practice and its share of Southern QRA duties, until the end of April, when it relinquished ops duties and ran down in strength.

During May many of the Squadron's pilots delivered examples of the unit's Lightnings to various airfields in the UK and overseas, for Battle Damage Repair training, 'gate guardian' duties, or preservation. Wg Cdr Jake Jarron left the Squadron on 25 May, and was succeeded as CO by Sqn Ldr John Aldington (previously 'B' Flight Commander), who had the distinction of making the final RAF Lightning flight on Thursday 30 June 1988 when he

Below:
F6 XS934 'K', complete with overwing tanks, at Leuchars in 1967. *Author*

Above:
Wg Cdr Jake Jarron's black-finned beauty XS903 'BA' at Binbrook on 17 March 1988 during 'Mallet Blow'. A broken refuelling probe later caused an early return to base.
John Dunnell

delivered one of the last three F6s in company with the last three T5s, to Cranfield, Bedfordshire, where they were purchased by Australian millionaire entrepreneur Mr Arnold Glass, who hopes to keep at least two or three of these magnificent fighters flying.

Meanwhile, the four Lightning F6s operated from Warton by British Aerospace, XP693, XR724, XS904, and XS928, are scheduled to continue flying until at least 1990, and hopefully even longer.

Markings

The traditional black rectangle with superimposed yellow diamond was applied on each side of the nose roundel, with fin marking comprising a pair of buff-coloured eagles within a small white disc — to which a black outline was added from about March 1968; the code letter was black.

Not long after the move to Binbrook in 1972 the fin markings were changed to a large pair of black eagles, with white, brown and yellow detail.

The next stage came on 18 August 1975 when XS452, a Lightning T5 of 'C' Flight, flew for the first time after the application of an experimental Dark Green matt camouflage to the upper surfaces (the undersurfaces remaining in the previous natural metal finish). This was the first UK-based operational Lightning to be camouflaged, and featured red and blue roundels of reduced diameter, and smaller black and yellow markings on the nose. Fin markings consisted of the large black eagles, which were outlined in yellow, and the code letter 'Y' was also yellow. This aircraft retained the green finish for more than 18 months, but in that time it had successively acquired LTF markings, then back to No 11 Squadron, coded 'T' in white, and by the end of 1967 it was repainted grey and green,

which by then was the standard camouflage scheme.

Single then double code letters remained in white on No 11 Lightnings, and the only significant change in markings related to those aircraft which were painted in the various 'air superiority' shades of grey, when the squadron markings were reduced in size and moved to the fin, on each side of a yellow disc containing the pair of black eagles.

A noteworthy variation in code letters occurred in 1984 when the two F3s assigned to provide the Strike Command Lightning solo aerobatics display during the air show season were XR718 coded 'BK1' and XP749 (the reserve aircraft) 'BK2', in each instance the numeral being much smaller than the letters.

In the summer of 1986 the pale grey aircraft 'belonging' to the CO, Wg Cdr Jake Jarron, XR725 'BA', was decorated with a black fin and spine. Towards the end of 1987 its fatigue life was running low and it was replaced as 'Bravo Alpha' by another pale grey F6, XS903, in the same scheme but with the large brace of eagles on the fin.

19 SQUADRON

Throughout its entire history No 19 has been a fighter squadron, since it was established at Filton, Bristol, in June 1916 with BE12s. It took these to France the following month, before re-equipping with Sopwith Dolphins in 1918 — the first squadron to do so, and henceforth the dolphin has been incorporated in its official badge. It was chosen as the first operational Lightning F2 squadron.

No 19 was the first Lightning squadron to benefit from the newly-available T4 dual-control trainer version to assist in the conversion process from 720mph Hunter to 1,500mph Lightning, and it was therefore hardly surprising that the first aircraft to be delivered to its base at Leconfield, in the East Riding of Yorkshire, was a T4, XM988, which arrived on 29 October 1962. In fact a quartet of these T-birds arrived at the base between then and Christmas; some were on loan or destined for other units, but all were used to assist the conversion process for the Leconfield Wing, where a working party from BAC was also present to help ensure a smooth transition. XN 775 was flown in to the airfield from Warton on 17 December as the first F2 for No 19 Squadron where it was coded 'D', and by the spring the full complement of 12 fighters and one trainer was established.

By the summer of 1963 No 19 was declared fully operational and took its place within the UK air defence network. On 14 September several of the squadron's F2s made their public debut at the 'Battle of Britain' open days held at different RAF stations. With serviceability steadily improving, the number of sorties flown during the month of October increased to 375.

In January 1964 the squadron concentrated on flight-refuelling practice from Valiant tankers preparatory to the special deployment in March of three F2's, XN 730'B', 778'F' and 781'J', to Saudi Arabia. This was a discreet detachment, staged through Bahrain, where all markings were removed from the aircraft before they flew on to their final destination: their purpose was to demonstrate the Lightning to an evaluation team from the Royal Saudi Air Force, which resulted in orders.

Gaining from this experience of overseas travel, No 19 sent a larger contingent of F2s to Luqa, Malta, in June the same year, where they took part in exercises which tested the island's defences. 1965 saw the squadron selected to conduct the first full-scale service in-flight refuelling trials from the new Victor K1 tankers, which after a gap of several months had replaced the hastily-withdrawn Valiants found to be suffering serious fatigue problems.

By the end of the spring, most of No 19's Lightnings were operating in the four-gun configuration, and

Top:
A rare photograph of one of three No 19 Squadron Lightning F2s, XN778 'F', which visited Saudi Arabia in March 1964 to be demonstrated to RSAF air staff. It is pictured at Bahrain, where all the markings were removed, and then reapplied upon return. (The other two aircraft were XN730 'B' and XN781 'J'.) *Gordon Macadie*

Above:
F2 XN782 'K' of No 19 Squadron overflying its base at Gütersloh, circa 1967. *Gunther Kipp*

Below:
Airbrakes out, 1½sec from touchdown at Gütersloh, is XN735 'A', an F2A of No 19 Squadron circa 1970. Note the symmetric nose chequers. *Gunther Kipp*

Above:
T4 XM991 'T' of No 19 Squadron in its final camouflaged decor. *Martin Horseman*

engaged upon limited ground attack training over the East Coast weapons ranges. This was in preparation for the transfer of the Leconfield Lightning Wing to RAF bases in West Germany, where their prime task would remain air defence, but as part of the 2nd Tactical Air Force it was desirable to possess some experience in strafing ground targets. No 19 left Yorkshire on 23 September 1965 and took up residence at RAF Gütersloh, less than 100 miles from the border with Soviet-occupied East Germany.

Although the prime duty of intercepting unidentified aircraft which strayed into Allied air space was essentially the same as in the UK, tactics were revised. Because of the Lightning's outstanding rate of climb and the proximity of the East German frontier, it was often more prudent to head west on the initial climb-out from Gütersloh, before turning at high altitude to patrol the border air identification zone. The situation was also quite different from the UK in that both NATO and Warsaw Pact forces could easily detect the other's air activity for considerable distances from the border, thanks to long range radar.

With the decision to convert most of the F2s to F2A standard (featuring the F6-type cambered wing and large ventral tank) the process of ferrying F2s to Warton for re-manufacture began late in 1966. Because there were virtually no spare aeroplanes it was quite a gradual process to avoid depleting the two German-based squadrons, and therefore the last F2A was not completed until July 1970. XN781 'B' was No 19's first F2A, delivered in February 1968, and by February 1970 when the squadron was at full strength its complement stood at 13 F2As, one F2 (used for target facilities) and one T4.

Increasingly the German-based Lightnings of Nos 19 and 92 Squadrons were employed on low-level intercep-

tion tasks, and to make them blend inconspicuously with the North German countryside a matt dark olive green camouflage paint was applied to the upper surfaces of these aircraft from 1972. The low-level flying had an adverse effect upon airframe fatigue, and despite recent major overhauls and rewiring of the aircraft's electrical systems by No 60 MU at Leconfield, it was decided to replace the Lightnings with Phantoms (based at Wildenrath). No 19 Squadron was the first to go on 31 December 1976, handing over some of its more youthful aircraft to No 92 which soldiered on for a few more months.

Markings

No 19 Squadron's markings were not as colourful as those of some other Lightning squadrons but they were consistent! From the outset the traditional Royal Blue and white chequers were applied each side of the nose roundel, five rows ahead of it and three rows aft. The winged dolphin marking was applied above the fin flash, with small black code letter near the fin tip.

The T4 XM988 (re-coded soon after delivery from 'O' to 'T'), carried the same markings as the F2's, with the exception of the yellow training bands around the rear fuselage and across each wing. From 1965 onwards these yellow markings were deleted from Lightning trainers.

The arrival of F2As was accompanied by a slight revision to the nose chequers, which were reduced in number to three rows on each side of the roundel to create symmetry. Fin markings remained substantially the same, although the dolphin was moved closer to the leading edge, and the code letter was slightly enlarged.

The introduction of camouflage caused a reduction in the size of the squadron insignia on the nose, and the individual code letter on the fin, 'though initially retained in black was later repainted yellow.

Below:
What a tribute to No 19 Squadron's engineers! All 13 of the unit's F2As plus an F2 are airborne in this picture — testimony to the Gütersloh ground crew's excellent serviceability. *Gunther Kipp*

No 23 Squadron

The history of No 23 Squadron began with its foundation on 1 September 1915 at Gosport, Hampshire. The squadron moved north from Coltishall to Leuchars, near St Andrews, in Fife, during March 1963 and less than 18 months later a 'new' No 23 Squadron was established there equipped with the Lighting F3, the squadron's first single-seat fighter type since 1933.

After delivery of the first pair of brand new Lightnings — XP707 and XP708 on 18 August 1964, further new F3s were received at the rate of more than one aircraft a week. The full squadron establishment of 12 fighters plus a T4 trainer was attained by the end of October, though No 23 was not fully operational until the New Year, taking its place alongside No 74 Squadron. Between them they constituted the RAF's premier fighter wing, equipped with the latest interceptor which at that time was indisputably the finest of its class in the world. Nevertheless, in the almost-daily encounters with the Soviet reconnaissance aircraft coming down through the 'Faroes Gap' the disadvantage of the Lightning F3's limited endurance became all too apparent to the Leuchars Wing while there was an absence of flight-refuelling tanker aircraft following the grounding of Valiants and the urgent modification of Victor bombers as tankers. To make good this critical shortfall the RAF was obliged to summon assistance from the USAF, which provided several KC-135s for this purpose, and the end of 1964 and beginning of 1965 saw both Nos 23 and 74 Squadrons busily engaged in inflight refuelling training and operational sorties off northeast Scotland.

On 3 June 1966 the T-bird, XS417 'Z', suffered Category 3 damage caused by a ground starting explosion and 23 had to borrow other T5s from No 226 OCU for many months because of this.

Above:
Old and new fighters of No 23 Squadron pose together in September 1965. Javelin FAW9R XH886 'G' in the foreground possessed four Firestreak missiles, four 30mm cannon, long endurance and a two-man crew. This compared with its replacement — the Lightning F3 — which was armed with only a pair of Firestreaks, but was twice as fast. XP756 'C' wears the white fin and spine paint scheme which decorated 23's first Lightnings. *MoD*

In May 1967 the squadron won the Dacre Trophy, and provided the Fighter Command Lightning solo aerobatics display that year. The display pilot chosen was Flt Lt Alan Turley, who had already been obliged to vacate his favoured aircraft, XP760 'K', on 24 August the previous year several miles off the Northumbrian coast, being picked up from the sea by a Whirlwind rescue helicopter. His replacement aircraft, XP705 'K', participated at the Paris Air Show. A few days later, still with its special Show identification number '90' on its nose, it was among 28 Lightnings from several squadrons which assembled at Wattisham for a mass flypast over London on 10 June to mark HM the Queen's Official Birthday.

May had also been a momentous month for No 23 when it started to receive Lightning F6s. A few of these were former No 5 Squadron Interim aircraft, supplemented by some full standard machines straight off the production line, including XS938 'E', the very last F6 to be built, which was

Below:
XR725 'A' was one of the No 23 Squadron Lightning F6s which flew non-stop to participate in the Toronto Air Show in August 1968. It is shown almost two weeks after its return, at Leuchars, on 14 September 1968, and still adorned with the 'Air Canada' fin zap but devoid of the Union flag which it wore atop the fin in Canada. This was one of several F6s modified for a while with two ventral strakes just ahead of the belly tank (which were later removed). Note also the small unit markings compared to those of the adorned fin era. *Author*

delivered from Warton on 28 August 1967. Many of the squadron's displaced F3s went to Wattisham to equip the newly formed No 29 Squadron. The Interim 6s were themselves replaced by full standard aircraft in the early part of 1968, and two of these, XR725 'A' and XS936 'B', made the first non-stop transatlantic crossing by Lightning on 27 August when they flew to Canada to take part in the Toronto Air Show, together with an RAF Vulcan bomber. Refuelled *en route* by Victor tankers, the flight took 7hr 20min, and was intended to act as a rehearsal for the 1969 Daily Mail Transatlantic Air Race (in which the RAF chose not to enter any Lightnings!). However, the trip was a good training exercise and 23's Lightnings were well received in Canada; and upon return to Leuchars on 3 September the pilots were deservedly greeted with a champagne reception.

Later the same month No 23 Squadron was declared operational with the Red Top missile, and went on to win the Aberporth Trophy in 1970 and 1971 for missile proficiency. Between 1969 and 1971 the squadron took part in several overseas exchanges and deployments to Belgium, Malta, the Canadian base at Bad Solingen in West Germany and, unusually, to Sweden, where they were the first RAF fighters to visit the

Above:
A No 23 Squadron Lightning in its element, shepherding a Soviet 'Bear' reconnaissance aircraft away from northern British airspace 'somewhere near the Faroes Gap'. XR753 'A' is the CO's aircraft and carries a Wing Commander's pennant beneath the cockpit.
MoD

country for more than 10 years. Weapons of a different sort were tested against the banner targets towed by No 85 Squadron Canberras early in 1971, when 23's Lightnings were first fitted with two 30mm Aden cannon in the forward section of the ventral fuel tank — which subsequently became a standard fit on F6s.

From early in 1972 after No 11 Squadron departed for Binbrook, No 23 was the sole Lightning unit at Leuchars, having absorbed the three Mk 1s of the Target Facilities Flight. Phantoms now held sway at this premier fighter base, but No 23 remained active until 31 October 1975 when most of its aircraft were transferred to the Binbrook units and its number plate was taken over by a new Phantom squadron which formed at Coningsby.

Markings

Not to be outdone by the black-finned Lightnings of No 74 Squadron, its rival at Leuchars, No 23 adopted white fins, decorated with a red and black eagle, with a black code letter beneath it. The

white extended the length of the spine, and the unit's traditional livery of blue/red/blue rectangles appeared each side of the roundel.

Following the edict to return to less flamboyant markings, the white fins and spines were supplanted in early 1966, and in their place a small red and black eagle was displayed on a white fin disc, and the black code letter moved nearer to the tip. A larger red eagle, with finer detailing in black and white, replaced the small fin disc by late summer 1970, and this style remained in vogue until the cessation of Lightning operations. In 1975 the CO's aircraft, XR753 'A', acquired an all-white fin and spine, and in so doing not only recalled the colourful markings of a decade earlier, but also created a precedent which was to be emulated by the COs of the Binbrook squadrons 11 years later!

The last of No 23's Lightnings to leave Leuchars was XS895, on 30 January 1976: it was specially 'zapped' with red and white 'Scottish Air Force' markings on its nose, and a pale blue/white St Andrew's cross on its fin.

Below:
Lightning T4 XM997 on finals to Middleton St George on 11 July
1963. This *very* rare photograph shows the 'last three' type of
code numbers in use even before the adoption of the red and
white No 145 Squadron markings.   *Alfie M. Alderson*

Bottom:
The first prototype P11, alias Lightning T4 XL628, sunning itself
at Farnborough in September 1959, less than a month before it
ended up in the Irish Sea on its 94th flight, after English Electric
test pilot J. W. C. Squier successfully ejected.   *John G. Johnson*

Below:
Lightning T4 XM997 on finals to Middleton St George on 11 July
1963. This *very* rare photograph shows the 'last three' type of
code numbers in use even before the adoption of the red and
white No 145 Squadron markings.   *Alfie M. Alderson*

No 29 SQUADRON

In April 1967 the Lightning F3s of No 56 Squadron began to arrive at Akrotiri from Wattisham to take over the defence of Cyprus from No 29 Squadron's Javelins. These returned to Wattisham where they were disposed of, and on 1 May a new No 29 Squadron re-formed with Lightning F3s at the same airfield. Initially only three or four F3s (left by the departing No 56 Squadron) were available, but early in May, No 29 received its first new Lightning, T5 XV328, fresh from No 60 MU. Establishment built up with the arrival of more F3s formerly used by Nos 23 and 74 Squadrons at Leuchars, which had become surplus after those units had begun to equip with F6s.

By September 1967 No 29 was operational, and on 18 May 1968 when Wattisham held one of its rare 'open days' the squadron was able to demonstrate its proficiency when it combined with its rival, No 111 Squadron, in a memorable stream take-off and 'threading the needle' tail chase by a dozen Lightnings which added their own thunder to the imminent electrical storm which soon engulfed the airfield. Later in the afternoon No 29 put up a precision aerobatics demonstration by four of its F3s.

While most of its time was spent on practice interceptions and exercises off the Suffolk coast, the squadron also had its share of overseas trips, which included Malta, France, Germany, Italy

Above:
No 29's only brand new Lightning, T5 XV328 'Z', shown here with the unit's early 'short' nose markings, and lacking the scarlet outline to the fin disc. '328 was among the last active T5s, being 'BZ' with No 11 Squadron in April 1988 — nearly 21 years after this photograph was taken. *MAP*

and Norway, some of which were exchange visits with fighter units from those countries. When Wattisham's runway was resurfaced No 29 was temporarily detached to Coltishall in July 1969, then Binbrook in October, before briefly returning home in December prior to a flight-refuelled redeployment exercise to Cyprus early in the New Year, where the squadron conducted live gunnery practice before returning to the UK.

No 29's time with Lightnings lasted little more than seven years, the shortest of any operational squadron. It was disbanded as such on 31 December 1974 and its number plate taken over by a newly-formed Phantom FGR2 squadron at Coningsby.

Markings

No 29's famous 'extra strength' (brewery) markings were applied to each side of the nose roundel, comprising white rectangles, outlined in red, and containing 'XXX' in red. Within the white fin disc there was an adaptation of the squadron badge consisting of a red eagle attacking a yellow buzzard. The aircraft code letter was black towards the tip of the fin. Early in 1968 the nose rectangles were elongated, and the fin disc was outlined in red.

Below:
You can almost smell the burning rubber in this shot of XP757 'M' touching down at Wattisham, photographed from another Lightning. Note the elongated nose markings. *BAe*

NO 56 SQUADRON

In common with most of the squadrons which flew Lightnings, No 56 had an illustrious history which began at Gosport; founded there on 8 June 1916, it soon followed the others to France and was engaged in bitter air fighting with its SE5 single-seat biplanes. No 56 will be remembered for two of its most distinguished World War 1 pilots — Capt Albert Ball who scored 44 victories before being posthumously awarded the VC, and Capt James McCudden, who also won the VC and ended the war with a tally of 57 victories.

With the delivery of XM172 'S' to Wattisham on 14 December 1960, No 56 became the first operational user of the Mk 1A version of the Lightning, which differed from the F1 mainly in having UHF radio from the outset, and in being 'plumbed' for in-flight refuelling. It was the spring of 1961 before the squadron had its full establishment of 12 Lightnings, and a temporary move to Coltishall due to runway repairs at its home base was to intervene during its work-up to operational status.

In 1962 the squadron began to exploit its air-refuelling capability with both wet and dry contacts with Valiant tankers over the UK. On 23 July two of the unit's Lightnings flew non-stop from Wattisham to Akrotiri in 4hr 22min, thanks to in-flight refuelling from Valiants of Nos 90 and 214 Squadrons *en route*, while on 4 October four more of 56's aircraft repeated the journey to demonstrate the pilots' proficiency in this, henceforth, essential requisite of Lightning squadrons.

For No 56 Squadron 1963 proved to be a momentous year, though tinged with sadness, when it was selected to succeed No 74 as the Fighter Command squadron aerobatic team. This accolade called for a complete colour scheme revision, and No 56 adopted scarlet fins, spines and leading edges to wings and tailplanes to produce arguably the most attractive livery ever donned by Lightnings. Entitled the 'Firebirds' (an appellation derived from the unit's rising phoenix emblem), and led by the CO, Sdn Ldr David Seward, the nine Lightnings put on such spectacular shows that it is hard to realise the team reigned for just a single season.

Exploiting the terrific acceleration and excellent power-to-weight ratio of the Lightning, the 'Firebirds' are likely to be remembered for their stream take-off and steep rotation climb followed by a twisting turn to bring them swooping down back over the airfield at low level, with reheats ablaze, before joining up for their precision formation flying at a more sedate pace.

A fact which is generally not known is that the AI23 radar sets were removed from 56's Lightnings for the three to four months of the 1963 air display season, and replaced by (red painted) lead weights bolted inside the radome. Although the squadron supposedly remained fully operational all the while it fulfilled its 'Firebirds' aerobatics schedule, this was hardly possible without any radar in the aircraft!

A number of 'Firebirds' pilots were former members of either No 92 Squadron's 'Blue Diamonds' Hunter aerobatic team or the 'Tigers' team flown by No 74 Squadron, and it was one of the latter, Flt Lt Mike Cooke, who sustained serious injuries during his ejection from XM179 'J' when it collided with XM174 'D' during a team rehearsal over Wattisham on 6 June 1963.

The summer of 1964 saw No 56 temporarily deployed to Coltishall again while Wattisham's runway received attention. Early in 1965 the squadron began to re-equip with Lightning F3s, for which yet another dramatic new colour scheme was devised.

Below:
The first style of markings on 56's F1s, with the pale blue fin disc containing the phoenix badge, and the small fin code. *Flight*

Top Left:
Even No 56 Squadron surpassed itself with its scarlet and white chequerboard decor used throughout 1965 by its F3s, seen here on XR718 'C' above the clouds. *via Gunther Kipp*

Centre Left:
Lightning livery in its heyday, 1965, is depicted in this magnificent photograph showing F2 XN779 'G' of No 19 Squadron nearest the camera, followed by F3 XP746 'K' of No 56 Squadron, F3 XP739 'H' of No 111 Squadron and F2 XN783 'A' of No 92 Squadron.

Below:
After the LCU became No 226 OCU at Middleton in June 1963 and assumed the identity of No 145 (shadow) Squadron, the unit's Lightnings adopted this most attractive red and white livery, seen on F1 XM143 on 15 October 1963.
Alfie M. Alderson

Top right:
Eight miles over West Germany on combat air patrol, this No 19 Squadron Lightning F2A was photographed from another of the species flown by Flt Lt Tony Paxton, in the spring of 1975.

Bottom right:
Strong cross winds at its Leconfield base prevented No 92 Squadron from flying its Lightning F2s on the July 1964 day when XN786 'D' was photographed. It wears 'second stage' markings when the blue was extended from the fin to the dorsal spine (still absent from its companion on the line), and the red and yellow nose markings lacked the white outline, added by September. *Roger Lindsay*

Revised No 56 Squadron markings comprising the larger phoenix and code letter, evident on XM171 'R'. *Author's Collection*

Below:
The 'Firebirds' scheme of No 56 Squadron's aerobatic team was arguably the most attractive of the many colours carried by lightnings. This line-up is headed by T4 XM989 'X'. *BAe via Andy and Hedley Molland*

Left:
Magnificent colours, which defied belief as a scheme for RAF fighters when first seen! Red and white chequers completely covered the fin, and 56 even dispensed with national insignia, as well as moving the code letter to the unique location of the airbrakes. F3 XR719 'D' made its stunning debut at Lakenheath USAF Armed Forces Day on 22 May 1965. *Author*

Dispensing with the conventional chequered nose markings in preference to a modern stylised arrowhead design, the main change was to the fin, which was completely covered in red and white chequers. Although it delighted the air enthusiasts, it attracted the displeasure of those in high places, and caused the toning down of all RAF fighter squadron markings from January 1966 following a Defence Council Instruction. Just before this occurred, the squadron contributed one of its colourful F3s, XP765 'N', to the 'Unison 65' display at Cranwell in September; and it was unusually fitted with dummy over-wing fuel tanks. The following year No 56 took part in the Malta air defence exercises, with little idea that within a few months it would be based in the Mediterranean. The move began on 11 April 1967 and was completed by May when the squadron's 13 F3s and single T5 took up residence at Akrotiri to replace the Javelins of No 29 Squadron. It had not been in Cyprus long before being put on full Battle Flight alert to preserve the integrity of British bases on the island when the Turks invaded to seize territory from the Greek Cypriots.

Soon afterwards three Canberras which had been provided for target towing and target facilities work were actually transferred to No 56 Squadron and acquired red and white chequerboard markings. The next change in equipment occurred in August 1971 with the delivery of Lightning F6s from Singapore following the disbandment there of No 74 Squadron. These aircraft superseded 56's F3s, and saw some intensive combat air patrols in December 1974 when the British Sovereign Base areas were again threatened by clashes among rival Cypriot factions.

Next month No 56 returned to the UK once again, taking up residence at Wattisham, where some ground crews and Lightning spares and servicing equipment had remained subsequent to the recent disbandment there of Nos 111 and 29 Squadrons. In June 1975 No 56 Squadron celebrated its diamond jubilee and its success in winning the Dacre Trophy that year, immediately prior to disbandment as a Lightning squadron on the 28th of the month.

Markings
Red and white chequerboard markings, thinly outlined in pale blue, and positioned asymmetrically with four sets

Below:
T5 XS422 was withdrawn from EPTS use during the latter part of 1987, fatigue-expired. *John Oaten*

of chequers forward of the roundel and one set aft, were applied to No 56's first Lightnings, which also featured the unit's red and yellow phoenix badge within a small pale blue disc just ahead of the fin flash. The individual aircraft letter was also quite small, and painted in black towards the tip of the fin, and, unusually for Lightnings, repeated on the back of the nosewheel door.

In 1962 the fin markings were revised by the substitution of a much enlarged and finely detailed phoenix badge; and a larger code letter, repositioned further down the fin. The following year the 'Firebirds' scarlet livery was introduced, which featured a third version of the phoenix. This was now set within a large white disc on the fin, just behind the enlarged, swept-back flash, which was relocated to the fin leading edge. The opportunity was taken to re-code the aircraft sequentially by serial number; the style of code letter was changed too, and outlined in white.

Re-equipment with F3s brought the flamboyant red and white chequered fins and arrowhead nose markings already mentioned, while individual aircraft code letters, red outlined in white, were positioned on the rear fuselage airbrakes. After 'toning down' treatment from January 1966 onwards, the red and white nose chequers, outlined in light blue, were reinstated, but this time symmetrically placed, with three sets on each side of the roundel. Fin markings reverted to a style similar to those first used by the F1s, with red and yellow phoenix within a pale blue disc, and a black code letter towards the fin tip. Finally, late in 1970, a much larger phoenix badge was stealthily introduced, and this remained in vogue until No 56 disposed of the Lightnings.

Top:
New and old: factory fresh F3 XR716 'D' in red and white chequerboard fin shares the Wattisham hardstanding with one of its predecessors, F1A XM176 'F' in 'Firebirds' scheme, early in 1965. *Geoff Parselle via Andy Molland*

Above:
There was a subsequent toning-down treatment of schemes, as featured on 56's T5, XS456 'A', at Wattisham. The small nose chequers, and fin markings and code, are reminiscent of the F1As. *Geoffrey Parselle via Ian White*

Below:
Another shot of T5 XS456, by now (1971) coded 'X' and based at Akrotiri. Note the white dorsal spine section to keep the avionics cool, and large phoenix fin badge. *Andrew Thomas*

XM163 'Q' was one of four F1s borrowed by No 74 Squadron from the AFDS to enable it to put up an aerobatic team in 1961. '163's true identity was 'H' AFDS.
Geoff Cruickshank

In September 1962 the 'Tigers' adopted the black fin and spine for their Lightning F1 aerobatics team. XM137 'D' is a former AFDS machine, seen at Coltishall in 1963.
Author's Collection

NO 74 SQUADRON

Among the most famous of RAF fighter Squadrons, No 74 was founded at Northolt on 1 July 1917 and remained in England for six months before being 'blooded' in France. Known as the 'Tigers', on account of its tiger face badge and its aggressive fighting spirit, No 74 also fought with distinction in the Battle of Britain.

No 74 moved to Coltishall in June 1959, preparatory to it becoming the first squadron to operate Lightnings and the only one fully equipped with the F1 variant. XM165, the first Lightning allocated to No 74 Squadron, was first delivered by English Electric test pilot Jimmy Dell on 29 June 1960, to Leconfield and into the custody of the CFE's Air Fighting Development Squadron, which was detached there while re-surfacing of Coltishall's runway was completed. The AFDS was at that time the RAF's only Lightning operator, with half-a-dozen of the aircraft in use for service evaluation and training. No 74 had to await the return of the AFDS to Coltishall on 11 July before receiving XM165, which returned as one of a five-ship AFDS formation that day.

Three days later No 74's South African CO, Sqn Ldr J. F. G. Howe, flew XM165, and by 22 July all the squadron pilots on the first phase of the conversion had flown at least one Lightning sortie — usually accompanied by a Hunter T7 in which a Lightning instructor provided practical and morale assistance by radio, since it was to be three years before two-seat, dual-controlled Lightnings entered service. Conversion proved surprisingly straightforward, despite the fact that the Lightning was twice as fast as the Hunter F6 it replaced, and had three times the rate of climb and even greater acceleration! This occasioned the now renowned comment from a No 74 Squadron pilot upon completion of his first Lightning flight: 'Superb — I was with it all the way until I let the brakes off.'

Not only had the squadron to cope with this quantum leap in performance and absorb the complexities of a weapons system, but it had to do so in the full glare of media publicity and a constant stream of visitors, who included Freddie Page and the C-in-C Fighter Command. Nonetheless, on 1 September, six of 74's Lightnings were flown to Boscombe Down to operate from there while taking part in the SBAC Show at Farnborough. On all but one (bad weather) day a four-ship formation was staged, led by the CO with Flt Lts A. W .A. 'Lefty' Wright (a former No 92 Squadron Sabre and Hunter aerobatic pilot) and Jeremy Cohu, and Flg Off Ted Nance, whose brother Tim later joined No 74. With the delivery of XM167 'H' on 26 September the squadron received its full quota of 12 F1s, and by January all 16 pilots were deemed to be operational on Lightnings.

In May the squadron concentrated on formation flying in preparation for its appearance at the Paris Air Show in June 1961, but was hampered by poor serviceability caused by lack of spare parts — a logistics problem which was to recur at several periods during the Lightning's lengthy service with the RAF! Nevertheless the squadron engineers worked wonders and, operating from Criel in Northern France, No 74's Lightnings impressed the crowds, as they were to do at many more air shows. The task of flying a nine-aircraft formation from a total establishment of 12 when serviceability remained a problem was temporarily overcome by drawing on the Lightning F1s of the AFDS which shared Coltishall, and between July and September, four AFDS machines were painted in No 74 Squadron markings, and used as reserves to bolster strength for the Farnborough SBAC Show and several Battle of Britain displays.

More displays were given in 1962, when as the 'Tigers' No 74 was appointed the official Fighter Command aerobatic team under its new CO, Sqn Ldr Pete Botterill, standardising on a seven-ship formation to minimise serviceability problems! On 24 May, staging through Karup in Denmark, eight 'Tigers' visited the Royal Swedish Air Force base at Vasteras, and after giving several shows in different parts of Sweden, returned via Norway on 6 June. During the last week of August 1961 the fins and spines of the aircraft were painted black as a prelude to participation at the Farnborough Air Show, which included synchronised aerobatics with No 92 Squadron's 16 'Blue Diamond' Hunters.

In March 1963 several of No 74's aircraft departed for overhaul at No 60 MU and were then issued to No 226 OCU, while the deficiency was only partly made up by the acquisition of ex-AFDS and trials F1s. On 28 January 1964, after 18 years in the Norwich area, No 74 moved 250 miles north to make Leuchars its new base, and with the arrival of XP700 'A' on 14 April the Squadron became the first to re-equip with Lightning F3s. By June almost all F1s had departed for second line duties. On 28 July the first public appearance of one of the new F3s was given at the Naval Air Day held at RNAS Lossiemouth when Flt Lt Glyn Owen gave a sparkling display of aerobatics. Glyn

Above:

F6 XR773 was photographed in yellow primer between resprays, at Binbrook in May 1981. *Terry Senior*

Below:

These rarely illustrated experimental No 5 Squadron markings were tried on Lightning F6 XS898 'J' in the summer of 1978 but not adopted. *Dave Tuplin*

elow:
harksteeth markings are shown to advantage on the 'famous' '6 XR770 'AA' of No 5 Squadron in October 1984. *Terry Senior*

Bottom:
The last Lightning to leave Leuchars, F6 XS895, taxying out for take-off on 3 February 1976 en route to Binbrook. This rare photograph shows the specially-applied nose and fin decor, which was removed upon arrival in Lincolnshire.
M. C. Bursell via Fred Martin

July 1966 saw No 74 Squadron hosting the annual 'Tiger Meet', when six NATO fighter units either named 'Tiger' or with a tiger in their badges visited Leuchars between 5 and 9 July. On 1 August No 74 took delivery of XR768 'A', and in so doing became the first operational squadron to be equipped with the full production standard Lightning F6, though it was a slow process and several of the new replacements were not delivered until December, when four were detached to Cyprus for two months of weapons training.

In March 1967 intensive arrester hook trials took place at Leuchars involving No 74's aircraft, which were fitted with a spring-loaded hook, flush with the rear fuselage, to engage a wire stretched across the runway 400yd from the up-wind end. Known as the RHAG (Rotary Hydraulic Arrester Gear), it was designed to prevent the aircraft from over-shooting the runway in the event of brakes or braking 'chute failure, and was subsequently fitted to late marks of Lightning.

On Sunday 4 June 1967 the CO, Wg Cdr Ken Goodwin, led the first of the squadron's 13 Lightning F6s from Leuchars to the unit's new base for the next four years, RAF Tengah in Singapore, where it was fully operational

Top:
Photographed after 74 removed to Leuchars is T4 XM974 with yellow 'T' band overpainted across the base of the black fin. *Andrew Thomas*

Above:
Hot metal! With larger, asymmetric nose markings, and fin flash (outlined in yellow) swept back and moved to the leading edge, No 74 Squadron's Lightning F3s were the fastest operational fighters in the West when they entered service in the summer of 1964. The starboard wing roundel is already flaking on XP705 'K', during an early outing off the Fife coast, flown by Flt Lt Henry R. Ploszek, a former No 56 Squadron 'Firebirds' aerobatic pilot, and at present Team Manager of the 'Red Arrows' aerobatic team, still flying fast jets. *MoD*

was an experienced fighter pilot who had already survived several emergencies, including ejection when he flew Sabres with No 66 Squadron 10 years earlier, and so it was particularly tragic when he was killed while practising low level aerobatics in XP704 'H' on 28 August at Leuchars while rehearsing for the station's Battle of Britain open day in September.

In April 1965 the squadron was involved in F3 in-flight refuelling operational trials — a new experience for

No 74 since their earlier F1 Lightnings lacked this capability. The same month a detachment flew to Wittmundhaven to operate with a Luftwaffe F-104 unit. On 3 June the Squadron Standard was presented to No 74 by HRH Princess Margaret, while in August 'A' Flight deployed to Cyprus, to be followed by the rest of the squadron in late September. During its stay in the Middle East No 74 paid a courtesy visit to Iran, which included a formation flypast over Tehran, for the Shah.

only 5 days later — the squadron's T5 having already arrived there earlier by sea. While in the Far East No 74's Lightnings took part in many air defence exercises, the most notable of which included 'Town House' on 16 June 1969, when four F6s flew to Darwin in Northern Australia, and 'Bersatu Padu' in August 1970, a five-nation multi-service affair in which the squadron's F6s proved their complete superiority in the air defence role. A year later the RAF withdrew from Singapore and No 74 disbanded on 25 August 1971. It ferried its aircraft to Cyprus for No 56 Squadron a few days later.

Markings

The squadron's distinctive black and yellow tiger stripe 'dicing' markings were applied each side of the nose roundel; interestingly, on the first aircraft, XM165, these markings were initially of the opposite pattern to that which became standard on all subsequent F1s. A large tiger's head set within a white disc adorned the fin, with the aircraft code letter, in black,

towards the fin tip. The four AFDS Lightnings lent to No 74 Squadron in the summer of 1961 (XM163 'Q', XM135 'R', XM136 'S', XM137 'T') carried identical markings.

During the last week in August 1962, the fins and spines of the aircraft were painted semi gloss black, and the code letter colour was changed to yellow. The same scheme was applied to T4, XM974 'T' after its transfer from the AFDS on 2 August, but it retained yellow training bands which made it even more eye-catching.

With the departure of some of its F1s for No 226 OCU in the spring of 1963 the remaining aircraft were re-coded in sequence with their serial numbers, eg XM134 'A', XM135 'B', XM136 'C', but the markings remained unchanged, except in the case of XM134, the CO's aircraft, which had a black fin but retained a natural metal spine. Following the visit to No 74 during April 1964 of the Hunters of No 325 Squadron, Royal Netherlands Air Force, the fin of at least one Lightning (XM135 'B') acquired that unit's large scorpion badge, and retained these markings until after its transfer to No 226 OCU.

With the Lightning F3s came the opportunity to add further refinement to the black fin scheme by moving the fin flash to the leading edge of the fins, and outlining it in yellow; the greatest change, however, involved the nose markings, which were considerably increased in size, and positioned asymmetrically with eight segments ahead of the roundel and four behind it.

Squadron esprit de corps was so strong at this time that most aircraft even had yellow dicing added to their black refuelling probes! With the instruction to standardise on more sober squadron markings in January 1966 the black decor was removed, and the fin disc containing the tiger's head emblem was reduced to a mere 18in diameter; the code letter was black. With the introduction of F6s a variation in the nose markings was experimentally tried on several aircraft in the autumn and winter of 1966: these comprised fewer, larger dicing segments, which were of equal width on each side of the roundel. Examples of this style included F6s XR770 'C', XR771 'D', XR773 'F', and T5 XS416 'T', but it was abandoned in February 1967 in favour of the earlier format. The final form of markings came in 1968 with the re-introduction of black fins (but not spines) and yellow code letters.

Below:
The photograph captures a take-off at Gan Island in the Indian Ocean, as 74's F6s are ferried back from Singapore to Cyprus for No 56 Squadron. *Geoff Parselle*

Above:
XS903 'BA' succeeded XR725 towards the end of 1987 as No 11 Squadron CO's aircraft. Its revised markings comprised a large pair of eagles. *Flt Lt Ian Black*

Below:
In mid-1978 XS898 'J' of No 5 Squadron carried experimental markings, but had reverted to a conventional style when photographed later in the year. It carries overwing tanks as it refuels from a basket deployed from a USAF tanker's boom.
T. R. Paxton

NO 92 SQUADRON

No 92 Squadron was founded at London Colney on 1 September 1917 as a scout squadron.

Early in 1963 some of No 92's pilots began the Lightning Conversion Squadron course at Middleton, and then returned to Leconfield for further training on the base's T4s in readiness for the arrival of the unit's first F2, XN783, on 26 March, which soon became 'A'. Several more Mk 2s followed during April to enable No 92 to begin conversion training in earnest, but it was not until late June that the full establishment was received, operational status following soon afterwards. Air refuelling practice took place the following year, 1964, when No 92 was accorded the privilege of once again being appointed Fighter Command aerobatic team in succession to the 'Firebirds' of No 56 Squadron.

1965 began with continued operational training, and at times most of 92's F2s were configured with four 30mm cannon, the lower two guns displacing the pair of Firestreak missiles, enabling the Lightnings to participate in some air-to-ground gunnery practice over the East Coast weapons ranges. On 29 December No 92 left Leconfield for RAF Geilenkirchen in Germany, but another move was made in February 1968 to join No 19 Squadron at Gütersloh because it was more economic and practical to operate all the German-based Lightnings from one airfield, and also to share the Battle Flight readiness alert with each squad-

Above:
The squadron's T4, XM995 'T', shows the white outlined nose markings and all-blue spine, as well as yellow 'T' bands. *Geoff Cruickshank*

ron taking this duty in alternate months. Gütersloh kept two Lightnings at 5min readiness the whole year, day and night, and from the issuing of the order to scramble it was expected that the aircraft would be airborne within 3min 15sec, but in practice some times of less than 3min were often achieved. The Lightning's AI23 took about 5min to warm up, but this was completed while the aircraft was airborne and

being vectored towards the threat target.

Between 26 June 1968 (when XN773 'E' returned as No 92 Squadron's first Lightning F2A following re-manufacture at Warton) and July 1970 there was a gradual changeover to the newer mark. Generally both Nos 92 and 19 maintained excellent serviceability and flight safety. However, F2A XN730 'J' of No 92 suffered a main-

Below:
No 92 Squadron Lightning F2 XN733 'L' is seen at Leconfield on 9 July 1964 in its original form of markings. *Author*

wheel undercarriage retraction problem in September 1971, but rather than abandon the aircraft the pilot elected to stay with it and effect a landing at Gütersloh on the good mainwheel and nosewheel. This was achieved with considerable skill, the net result being comparatively little damage to the nose of the aircraft when touchdown speed fell off and the Lightning toppled over.

NATO exchange visits, usually within the Continent, occurred once a year, with each pilot attending the Missile Practice Camp (MPC) at Valley to fire a live Firestreak during his first year on the squadron. Unlike UK-based Lightning squadrons, Nos 92 and 19 Squadrons conducted their Armament Practice Camps (APC) for live gunnery at Decimomannu in Sardinia. The Gütersloh Lightnings used regularly to exercise with Marham-based Victor tankers, using an air refuelling zone over North Germany some 60 miles north of base; on Fridays the Victor(s) would often operate from Gütersloh itself to extend refuelling exercise time.

No 92's Lightnings adopted the dark olive green camouflage from 1972 until the conclusion of their operational service on 1 April 1977, after which several remained in use as non-airworthy decoys at Gütersloh and other RAF airfields in Germany and the UK.

Markings

A red and yellow arrowhead marking each side of the nose roundel graced 92's first Lightnings, which featured

Above:
An F2 in natural metal finish: XN788 'P' of No 92 Squadron just prior to the camouflage era. *Gunther Kipp*

the squadron emblem of a cobra entwined between two maple leaves, set against a white disc on the fin — which initially remained in natural metal finish on F2 XN783 'A' and T4 XM995 'T', each carrying the very small code letter in black at the top of the fin. While F2 deliveries were still incomplete the fin décor was changed to a Royal Blue background, white code letter, and the fin flash moved forward and raked back at the same acute angle as the leading edge.

The next change occurred in June 1964 when the blue fin was extended to cover the length of the dorsal spine. For the Farnborough Show in September a fine white outline was added to the nose markings and the roundel, and this remained the situation until 1968 when

the arrowhead markings were replaced by red and yellow chequers on each side of the nose roundel. This scheme continued on the F2A aircraft until late in 1971 when blue was removed from fin and spine, and the code letter was enlarged and painted black.

During the next year camouflage was introduced and nose markings were greatly reduced in size. Strangely, no change applied to the fin badge, although the code letter remained black for a while before amendment to yellow was felt necessary. In its last year with Lightnings the addition of two dark blue diamonds beneath the white fin disc was a reminder of 92's heyday with its Hunter aerobatics team. The CO's aircraft, XN793 'A', featured a small gold crown above the fin badge and the words KING COBRA on each side of the disc, while beneath the cockpit on the port side was written 'Flagship 92' in script.

Below:
The white puff of burnt rubber smoke has frozen the 170mph touch-down of this No 92 Squadron F2A, XN782 'H', at Gütersloh. *Martin Horseman*

NO 111 SQUADRON

'Treble One' Squadron stemmed from a Flight of No 14 Squadron, from which it formed on 1 August 1917 at Deir-el-Belah, Palestine. It was chosen as the first squadron to receive the Hawker Hurricane — the RAF's first modern fighter capable of speeds greater than 300mph in level flight — and in 1957 it became the official Fighter Command aerobatic team, painting its Hunter 6s glossy black. Thus began a three-year reign as the 'Black Arrows', building up from five aircraft to seven, and then more usually to a nine-aircraft formation, and in 1958 it performed a 22-aircraft loop — a feat which has never been surpassed.

'Treble One' began its association with the Lightning on 6 March 1961 when it took delivery of XM185 to become the third squadron to fly Lightnings, and the second to be equipped with the F1A version. During the next 14 years No 111 was to become unique in operating every Lightning variant except the Mark 2A.

Re-equipment with Lightnings was a somewhat protracted business because No 111 was virtually waiting for the

Above:

A rare shot of 111's first T4, XM973 'T', being loaded with a Firestreak acquisition round — note the hoist fitment beneath the wing root and the special missile trolley. *MoD via Andy Molland*

Below:

New decor for 'Treble One's' F1As appeared in the spring of 1964 resulting from a competition organised by the OC, Sqn Ldr George Black, and won by a member of the squadron's ground crew who prepared an Airfix model in his proposed scheme. XM184 was photographed at Alconbury Armed Forces Day, 23 May 1964. *Author*

aircraft to be built, barely a month elapsing between the first flight and delivery to Wattisham, with a number of essential production test flights by English Electric pilots sandwiched in between. The situation was not helped by the untimely loss of the first machine XM185, coded 'C', on 28 June 1961, after undercarriage problems which caused its pilot to eject safely after pointing it towards the disused airfield of Rattlesden, Suffolk. No 111's full complement was finally achieved on 29 August with the arrival of XM216 'P', coincidentally the last F1A to be built, after which the squadron's pattern of operational tasks was similar to that of No 56 Squadron, with which it shared a friendly rivalry at Wattisham. In 1962 'Treble One' gained proficiency in air-refuelling and during the next two years put this training to full use with several overseas detachments, including Cyprus and Malta. More unusually the squadron was also involved in operational flight refuelling trials in which No 111's Lightnings took on fuel from de Havilland Sea Vixen all-weather fighters of the Fleet Air Arm.

These activities were interspersed with an early deployment to RAF Gütersloh in West Germany, before returning to England to continue the normal round of duties. A variation from the norm occurred when 'Treble One' was assigned to participate in some high-altitude high-speed gun-firing trials. By 1963 the upper cannon ports on most Fighter Command Lightnings had been faired over to reduce drag and because of the reliance on the pair of Firestreak missiles as primary armament. (Incidentally the fairing plates used to cover the cannon varied enormously from squadron to squadron — some being very crudely fashioned in the station workshops and simply pop-riveted in place!) During these high-altitude gunnery trials above 35,000ft, 'Treble One's' Lightnings used only the two lower Aden guns, in a weapons pack which displaced the Firestreaks. This same configuration was employed in July 1964 when several of No 111's aircraft were deployed to Malta, and then flew on to RAF El Adem in Libya where they practised air-to-ground live gunnery at targets on a desert range, and reportedly also fired 2in rockets from an alternative weapons pack — a form of armament which was hardly ever used by Fighter Command.

Aircraft attrition had been higher than average, with several Lightnings written off in accidents, mainly due to technical problems. The net effect was such a depletion of No 111's strength that during the latter half of 1964 it borrowed aircraft from other squadrons, hence the reason it operated so many Lightning variants. The first of these were a pair of F2s which arrived from Leconfield at the end of May: XN778 'F' of No 19 Squadron stayed only a week, but XN788 'R' of No 92 Squadron was on strength until early June. The F2s were deemed unsuitable as they differed significantly from the F1A in respect of instrument layout and reheat and had a liquid oxygen breathing system.

The first production F1A, XM169, which had spent its previous career as a test aircraft, was allocated to No 111 Squadron on 14 October for extended loan — which was presumably the reason why it was never painted in the squadron's full markings, merely acquiring the yellow code letter 'B' and an attempt at the Jerusalem Cross insignia on its fin.

Between September and December three F1s were used by No 111 Squadron — all were former No 74 Squadron aircraft which became surplus after displacement by F3s. Of this trio, two were decorated in the full finery of 'Treble One' livery — XM140 'R' and XM146 'J'. Known on the squadron as 'Romeo' and 'Juliet', only certain pilots were allowed to fly them because the F1 had a different throttle control and a more rudimentary type of reheat system. For these reasons the F1s were rarely flown and spent much of their time with No 111 Squadron on QRA duty — with the hope they would never need to be scrambled for real, since they lacked in-flight refuelling!

During mid-October several of No 111's pilots were posted to Leuchars to help establish the newly-formed No 23 Squadron as it worked up to operational status with Lightning F3s, while at Wattisham. 'Treble One's' shortage of aircraft ceased to be a problem with the receipt of XP738 on 7 November 1964, which heralded its own re-equipment with F3s, allowing the disposal of its earlier Lightnings to commence in the New Year — 'Romeo' and 'Juliet' were despatched to No 33 MU at Lyneham where, sadly, they were salvaged for spares recovery then broken up in the summer of 1966.

Only four F3s had reached No 111 by the end of 1964 but the delivery of six more in January enabled re-equipment to proceed rapidly, and with the arrival of XP742 on 10 February 1965 the squadron had its full quota of a dozen. It wasted no time in putting them to use, contributing the leading box of four, still unmarked, F3s, to the salutory flypast formation of 16 Lightnings during the state funeral in London of Sir Winston Churchill on 19 January. By the spring, now wearing the squadron's eye-catching black and yellow livery, further formation flying was the order of the day in preparation for the Paris Salon where the squadron put up a 12-aircraft formation each day between 13 and 16 June, drawn from its total strength of 12 F3s and single T4, which was a tribute to the unit's ground crews to achieve maximum serviceability — even the 13th aircraft participated as an exhibit in the static display! Before the end of the month the squadron lost its first F3 in dramatic manner: Flt Lt A. J. R. Doyle was giving a solo display of aerobatics in XR712 'B' at the Exeter Air Day on

Right:
'Treble One's' nine-ship formations performed at several major air shows in 1965. Here is a tight diamond of eight F3s led by the squadron's T4, at Farnborough, expanded to include seven scarlet Gnats of the Red Arrows — we sadly no longer see such showmanship! *MoD via Andy Molland*

Below:
'Romeo', one of three F1s used by 111 to supplement its dwindling F1As in the latter half of 1964, is seen here at No 33 MU, Lyneham, in October 1966 when prematurely scrapped — note the incomplete 'Treble One' Jerusalem Cross. *MAP*

26 June when the No 1 engine caught fire and began to shed parts of the jet pipe; he headed back to his temporary base at St Mawgan in Cornwall, but was obliged to vacate the burning Lightning off Newquay, being safely rescued from the sea by an RAF Wessex helicopter. On 30 September No 111 lost its second F3, XP739 'H', which crashed five miles short of base after both engines flamed out. The pilot was Hedley Molland, for whom this was his second ejection from a Wattisham-based aircraft, having 10 years earlier had the distinction of ejecting higher and faster than any previous RAF pilot, when he abandoned his No 263 Squadron Hunter; Hedley went on to accrue a prodigious number of flying hours on Lightnings (over 3,400), including export variants.

Although the RAF quickly discarded the Baxter Woodhouse & Taylor pressure helmet specially designed for high-altitude Lightning operations (because pilots found it restrictive and most uncomfortable), this did not prevent the aircraft being flown considerably higher than the 60,000ft frequently quoted by official sources as the practical operational ceiling. In the late summer of 1965 Lightning F3s from the Wattisham Wing demonstrated the aircraft's outstanding rate of climb and high-altitude performance by successfully intercepting very high-flying American Lockheed U-2 reconnaissance aircraft which were at that time operating from RAF Lakenheath, Suffolk — to the consternation of the USAF which had believed that these 'spy-planes' were immune to fighter interception.

In the latter part of July 1969 'Treble One' operated from Binbrook while Wattisham's runways received resurfacing maintenance, and thereafter had its share of the usual operational tasks with regular deployments abroad to enliven the normal duties. It was while a section of No 111 Squadron was on an exchange visit to the French Air Force fighter base at Colmar that the pilot of XP752 'D' had a

Below:
What a beauty! Factory fresh F3 XP740 'J' in 111's attractive decor, summer 1965.
MoD via Andy Molland

miraculous escape when he collided with a French Mirage IIIE on 20 May 1971, sustaining damage to the nose and forward fuselage which distorted the cockpit, making it impossible to use the ejection seat; he managed to make a safe landing but the aircraft never flew again.

'Treble One's' last overseas deployment with Lightnings was to Luqa, Malta, in July 1974 when the squadron exercised in defence of the island. Included within the unit's establishment were three Lightning F6s acquired on 15 May from No 23 Squadron, and operated without the usual twin gun pack armament in the ventral tank (30mm Aden ammunition was in any case a rare commodity at Wattisham since none of the base's F3s carried guns!). The trio were used to give No 111's pilots experience in handling this heavier fighter variant, since a number of them were to be posted to the remaining F6 squadrons after 'Treble One' ceased Lightning operations on 30 September 1974.

Markings

The introduction of Lightnings brought with it a unique Lightning flash marking which remained constant throughout the squadron's operation of the type, and has since been perpetuated on No 111's Phantoms. Painted in the squadron's colours of black, outlined in yellow, the flash was applied each side of the nose roundel, while the unit's badge, the Cross of Jerusalem, also in yellow outlined in black and with black and red detailing, appeared on the fin. Forward of the cross was the aircraft code letter in black, thinly outlined in yellow.

In the spring of 1964 'Treble One's' new CO, Sqn Ldr George Black, wanting to improve the squadron's esprit de corps, instituted a competition to design new markings. This was won by an airman on No 111's groundcrew who made a plastic Airfix kit of the Lightning F1A and painted it in what

Above:
The final form of Treble One Lightning markings is shown on F6 XS895 'Z', one of three of this mark acquired from No 23 Squadron in May 1974 — large black fin disc, and swept fin flash on the leading edge. Note the absence of the gun pack in the ventral fuel tank. *MoD*

was selected as the winning scheme. The markings were highly distinctive and comprised a black fin and spine; the fin featured a broad yellow stripe parallel with the leading edge, containing the squadron badge within a central black disc, with black code letter above it. Additionally a yellow flash was painted on the dorsal spine immediately behind the cockpit. The CO's machine, XM184 'A' was the first so decorated and carried the squadron leader's pennant on the fin as well as the more usual position beneath the cockpit.

Re-equipment with the square-finned F3s caused only minor amendment to this livery, the salient difference being the removal of the national insignia flash to the fin leading edge in a narrow stripe, outlined in white.

Initially the code letter, in white outline format, was positioned at the

base of the fin trailing edge where the flash had originally been, but after several aircraft had been painted in this way, the decision was made to revert to a black code letter high on the broad yellow fin stripe. By early April 1965 only 'B' and 'C' still had white-outline code letters.

After 'the directive' in January 1966, full colour fin markings were removed, the CO's aircraft XR711 'A' being the last to retain them. Instead, the squadron crest was reproduced within the standard 18in diameter fin disc. In the spring of 1974, when the squadron was within six months of disposing of its Lightnings, new markings were bravely introduced! A large yellow Cross of Jerusalem centred within a black fin disc made its reappearance, and an enlarged flash adorned the leading edge of the fin in a last gesture to reflect former glory!

Below:
A final line up for 111's Lightnings at Wattisham on 30 September 1974. F3 XP754 'R' leading. *RAF Wattisham*

CENTRAL FIGHTER ESTABLISHMENT/AIR FIGHTING DEVELOPMENT SQUADRON/FIGHTER COMMAND TRIALS UNIT

A component of the Air Fighting Development Squadron, itself part of the Central Fighter Establishment, became the first service operator of the Lightning in December 1959 when three late examples of the pre-production batch, which closely equated to the F1, were delivered to Coltishall. XG334 'A' was the first to arrive on the 23rd, followed by XG335 'B' and XG336 'C' a few days after Christmas, and they, in common with all the subsequent marks of Lightning issued to the AFDS, were used to evaluate and devise operational tactics preparatory to the type entering squadron service. XG334 suffered a hydraulic failure which prevented the undercarriage from being lowered, and the pilot, Sqn Ldr Harding, had no alternative but to eject from the aircraft just off the Norfolk coast near Wells, on 5 March 1960, thereby achieving the dubious distinction of being involved with the first of very many RAF Lightnings which were written off in accidents.

On 25 May 1960 the AFDS took delivery of its first full production F1, XM135 'D' (destined to become quite a famous aircraft, and, coincidentally, the very last Mark 1 in RAF service before it was retired on 20 November 1974; it was flown from No 60 MU Leconfield to Duxford to become a worthy exhibit in the Imperial War Museum collection, with 1,343 flying

hours to its credit). It was followed to the AFDS by four more F1s which remained in use until early in 1963 when the survivors were transferred to No 74 Squadron, by which time they had been supplanted by F2s at the AFDS.

The next mark of Lightning to reach the AFDS was, however, the T4, two of which (XM973 'K' and XM974 'J') were delivered in August 1962 for service trials, dual checks and continuation training. XM973 stayed barely a year, while XM974 finally departed early in 1966 but was often loaned as a 'spare' to UK Lightning squadrons.

In October 1962 the CFE's small miscellaneous fighter fleet comprising Javelin FAW8s, Hunters and a few Meteor 'hacks' in addition to the AFDS Lightnings, made Binbrook its new base. There delivery of the RAF's first F2 Lightning, XN771 'M', for the AFDS occurred on 14 November, followed by four further examples including an attrition replacement for XN777 'N'. The latter had overshot the runway on 21 December and was extensively damaged when 'captured' by the Safeland netting barrier, the accident being somewhat of an embarrassment to the pilot, who was the Air Commodore boss of the CFE!

The AFDS's task of devising and testing tactics of all new fighter variants prior to their entry into operational squadron service meant

that it never needed more than a handful of each new type of Lightning nor did it keep them long, and so it was that by early 1965 the F2s had gone from Binbrook, their place taken by a quartet of F3s. XP695 was the first of these, delivered on 1 January 1964, and proved to be the last to leave on 4 July 1966. The F3s were supplemented, then replaced by Interim F6s commencing with XR753 'T', delivered on 16 November 1965. Shortly afterwards, on 1 February 1966, the AFDS became the Fighter Command Trials Unit, and on the 22nd of the month acquired XM164 'Z', the first of two Lightning F1s to be evaluated in the target facilities role.

30 June 1967 saw the disbandment of the FCTU and dispersal of its F6s to No 23 Squadron while the two F1s remained at the base to form the Binbrook Target Facilities Flight.

Markings
All marks of AFDS Lightnings carried a black code letter on the fin (although the T4s only briefly), the F1's featuring the unit crest within a black square on the fin, with the squadron's title in full beneath it. By 1961 dark red/black bars on each side of the nose roundel became the standard unit marking (though never applied to the T4s). On F2s, F3s and F6s the nose marking was outlined in white, while on the F2s a small disc marking was adopted on the fin.

Below:
F1 XM137 'F' of the AFDS in 1961, at Waddington. The nose markings were dark red and black bars, to which a white outline was added on AFDS F2s, F3s and F6s. *Author*

LIGHTNING CONVERSION SQUADRON/NO 226 OPERATIONAL CONVERSION UNIT

The LCS was formed at Coltishall on 4 January 1960 under the aegis of the CFE with the task of training Lightning pilots. To begin with only more experienced jet pilots with 1,000 flying hours were chosen to fly the new fighter, and some of those were retained as instructors, before the qualifications were relaxed to include younger pilots on their first squadron tour. The initial training was accomplished with various systems aids and a flight simulator, and because the LCS had no aircraft of its own, Lightnings were borrowed from No 74 Squadron and the AFDS which shared Coltishall.

In August 1961 the LCS moved north to Middleton-St-George and continued to borrow Lightnings, mainly from Nos 56 and 111 Squadrons. Usually only a single aircraft for a few days at a time was all that could be spared, but nevertheless the LCS was responsible for the successful conversion of several squadrons to Lightnings. Not until 27 June 1962 did the LCS receive its own aircraft when T4 XM970 was delivered to Middleton, soon coded 'G', and followed by a further seven before the end of October. 12 December saw the untimely end of XM993 which ran off the runway after landing at Middleton while returning from Chivenor; it turned over, caught fire and was burnt out, but fortunately after its two occupants had safely clambered out of the wreck.

On 1 June 1963 the LCS was re-titled No 226 OCU and shortly afterwards it received seven ex-No 74 Squadron F1 single-seaters, via No 60 MU where they had been overhauled. In August the OCU introduced a most attractive red and white livery which was based on the St George's Cross and reflected the unit's shadow identity in time of crisis as No 145 Squadron.

Being the main operator of two-seat Lightnings, No 226 OCU's T4s were in great demand to fly VIPs and other notables at speeds greater than 1,000mph and so qualify them to be members of the 'Ten Ton Club', complete with scroll and special tie. No 226 OCU made it possible for a distinguished lady pilot, Mrs Diana Barnato Walker from London, to become the first British woman to achieve that distinction on 26 August 1963, in XM996 flown by Sqn Ldr Ken Goodwin, the CO.

Having spent millions to transform Middleton-St-George into a Lightning base, the RAF sold the airfield for a mere £340,000 for civilian use as Teesside Airport, and on 13 April 1964 No 226 OCU's 14 Lightnings took off for their new home at Coltishall. A year later the unit received its first Lightning T5, XS419, on 20 April 1965, and by then it was already in the process of replacing its F1s with former Nos 56

56

and 111 Squadron F1As. From then on strength increased until the late 1960s when the OCU had 36 Lightnings on its inventory for a while, divided fairly evenly between the three versions, to which another was added from June 1970 onwards when about eight Lightning F3s were acquired. By then some of the F1As were periodically operated as targets, in much the same way as the TFF Lightnings, with the AI23 radar replaced with a Luneberg Lens to create a larger radar 'signature'.

From 4 May 1971 the three different squadrons within No 226 OCU were each given a stronger identity: No 1 was the Conversion Squadron, equipped with T4s and F1As, and adopted the markings of No 65 Squadron; No 2 was the Weapons Squadron, and used the same markings on its Lightnings, which also included T5s. Thirdly there was the Advanced Squadron, equipped with F3s and T5s, and early in October 1971 it introduced blue and white markings, which were at first thought to represent No 66 Squadron but were in fact soon revealed as No 2T Squadron.

Above:
65 and 2T markings superseded 145's, and both are shown on this OCU formation of F1A XM216, T4 XM997 and T5 XS419 '2T'. *MoD*

In 1973 and 1974 one of No 226 OCU's instructors, Flt Lt Peter Chapman, was the RAF's Lightning display pilot, and put up some scintillating performances, wherever possible flying his favoured mount, F3 XP696, which sported a white fin and dorsal spine in its final season. At the conclusion of September 1974, No 226 OCU was disbanded and many of its Lightning F1As and T4s were withdrawn from service and scrapped. The same fate befell XP696, possibly due to the airframe stress induced by Pete Chapman's rivet-popping performances!

Markings
The only identification of LCS ownership was a single black code letter on the fins of four of the Squadron's Lightning T4s, 'G', 'H', 'J' and 'K', from late July 1962. Deliveries after September remained totally anonymous until

Below and right:
No 65 and 2T markings in close-up. *Author*

Left:
No 226 OCU's toned down scheme on T5 XS457. *Brian Lowe*

the addition to the fin tip of 'last three' serial numbers in black, early in 1963. In June 1963 the appearance of the newly-created No 226 OCU Lightnings was transformed by the addition of red and white markings to dorsal spine and fin; the red leading edge segment of the arrowhead contained a white shield within which was a scarlet Cross of St George badge, with a sword diagonally superimposed. The last three numerals of the aircraft's serial number were painted in black just ahead of the nose roundel, in a square-cut style. The same décor was applicable to No 226 OCU's single-seat Lightnings, and to the T5s — which differed from the T4s in two respects: the training bands were fluorescent orange (instead of yellow), and extended over the leading edge of the fin.

In common with the removal of colourful markings from Lightnings, after 1965 those of the OCU gave way to No 145 Squadron's white rectangle with red cross insignia each side of the nose roundel, a miniature red cross fin disc, with the last three of the serial number re-located to the fin tip. In 1971 these were superseded by No 65 Squadron markings on T4s and F1As, while the T5s and F3s adopted the '2T' unit markings. The latter consisted of a pale blue diamond shaped marking, outlined in white, applied each side of the nose

Above:
XP696 in the white-finned scheme adopted by Pete Chapman. *Author*

roundel, and '2T' marking within the 18in diameter fin disc, plus the 'last three' serial number near the fin tip. The exception was Flt Lt Pete Chapman's F3 XP696 with all white spine

and fin. One other variation from the norm was T5 XS422 which had a large number '2' combined with the letter 'T' beneath it, in black, immediately above the fin flash.

Below:
A very rare shot of XS422 with one-off '2T' identification on fin. The aircraft later went to the ETPS. *Terry Senior*

LIGHTNING TRAINING FLIGHT

Formed at Binbrook at the beginning of October 1975 as the successor to 'C' Flight of No 11 Squadron, which was itself formed to continue the training of Lightning pilots after the disbandment of No 226 OCU in September 1974, the LTF was to enjoy a much longer lifespan and greater importance than was originally envisaged, due to the continually extended service life of the type.

Initial establishment was four each of F3s and T5s, though the number of T5s was occasionally increased. An F6 became a standard item from 1979 onwards, mainly for target facilities purposes, with a radar reflector usually fitted in lieu of the AI23 radar, and the all-fuel ventral tank to give it maximum endurance and training value.

The training pattern followed essentially the same general format as in No 226 OCU days, with new pilots arriving at the LTF from Tactical Weapons Units with fast-jet experience on Hawks. Wherever possible the new boy was given a T5 familiarisation ride on his very first day of arrival, to whet his enthusiasm for the Lightning, if any was needed. Two weeks of ground school followed, including about 14 'sorties' in the full-flight simulator which realistically conveyed the handling characteristics of either the F3 or F6 — a change effected merely with the flick of a switch!

Actual conversion training began with five flights in a T5, before the first solo in an F3, interspersed with further ground lectures. The first phase of conversion training culminated in concentrated flying up to Instrument Rating Standard, and then a series of exercises designed to broaden the student Lightning pilot's experience within quite a compressed time span including battle formation flying, before a Handling Test in a T5 to evaluate his progress. This was fol-

lowed by the weapons phase, featuring air combat training with Red Top acquisition rounds, and concluding with a final check ride, normally by the CO.

With about 42 Lightning flying hours in his logbook the new pilot was assigned to Nos 5 or 11 Squadrons, where his training continued until he was rated as fully operational. In addition to training new pilots, the LTF also ran various (shorter) refresher courses for Lightning 'retreads' before they resumed flying duties with either of the two front line squadrons at Binbrook.

The distinction of being the last pilot to be trained to fly the Lightning before the LTF disbanded in April 1987 went to Flt Lt Ian Black, who had previously been a navigator on Phantom FGR2s in Germany, and whose initial impressions of flying the Lightning are included later in this publication.

Markings

The first markings adopted by the Flight consisted of Royal Blue rectan-

gles on each side of the nose roundel, and a large blue lion (based on the Binbrook station crest) on the fin; the lion and the swept-back letters LTF above it were edged in red, and the lion had red and black detailing and yellow fleur-de-lis. To begin with no code letters were carried, but then were added to the base of the fin, in black on natural metal aircraft.

Shortly after its formation the LTF T5 XS458 was experimentally painted in Dark Sea Grey camouflage on its side and upper surfaces — to which the white code letter 'Z' was applied. The LTF later operated the experimental green camouflaged T-bird, XS452.

Grey and green camouflage was introduced later, and superseded on several LTF F3s, T5s and F6s by various 'air superiority' grey schemes adopted progressively by the Binbrook Lightning force from the early 1980s. These grey schemes were accompanied by the transfer of unit markings from the nose to the fin, with re-positioning of the code letters to the top of the fin.

To commemorate the LTF's 10th anniversary in October 1985, one of its grey F3s, XR749 'DA', was specially decorated with a dark blue dorsal spine and fin, embellished with an oversize lion within a white disc. In May 1986 the same aircraft was decorated in No 56 Squadron markings to commemorate that unit's 70th anniversary.

After the Flight had disbanded, some of its former Lightnings retained LTF markings for several months, during which they were operated by Nos 5 and/or 11 Squadrons.

LTF markings were even resurrected after the unit's demise: F6 XR728, a Dark Sea Grey machine, was 'adopted' by Gp Capt John H. Spencer, the Binbrook station commander, whose initials JS graced its fin.

TARGET FACILITIES FLIGHTS

After withdrawal from front line service, several Lightning F1s (soon joined by F1As) were overhauled, partially disarmed, mostly stripped of AI radar and fitted with a Luneberg Lens which increased the aircraft's radar reflection. Thus modified they were ready for their final, unglamorous but valuable task, as supersonic intercept targets.

Three Target Facilities Flights were established (each with two or three of these aircraft) to fulfil this function for the benefit of the F3/F6 operational squadrons, which were thereby saved depletion of their own aircraft and pilots for this purpose. The first pair of TFF aircraft were issued to the FCTU at Binbrook in February 1966, and when that unit disbanded in June 1967, became the Binbrook TFF; the other flights were based at Leuchars and Wattisham from 1966 until 1973.

Lightened by the removal of operational equipment and seldom flown with Firestreaks in place, except for air shows, these early machines were fast, light on the controls and well liked — XM144 in particular was referred to by the Boss of Wattisham TFF as the 'Queen of the Skies' in appreciation of its exceptional performance and handling.

The TFFs were disbanded on 31 December 1973 as an economy measure deemed necessary to avoid the provision of F1 spares at the three bases involved.

Markings — Binbrook TFF
A small Binbrook lion crest (blue) on a white fin disc; a black code letter high on the fin. Early in 1971 the TFF was absorbed by No 5 Squadron at the same base and wore its markings.

Top:
Binbrook TFF F1A XM169 'X' carries blue and white nose markings and Paris Salon number '1110' crudely painted on the nose, at Leuchars. *Bob Hobbs*

Above:
Leuchars TFF F1 XM139 retained its nose code from No 226 OCU use. The fin badge is based on the Station crest. *Author*

Leuchars TFF changed to yellow and red nose markings based on the Scottish flag.
Sqn Ldr J. M. Carder

In June 1972 F1A XM173 was delivered to Binbrook and operated by No 11 Squadron on TFF duties, though it is extremely doubtful if it ever carried that squadron's markings.

In September 1972 Binbrook TFF was reconstituted, and an imaginative design was submitted for the unit's new markings, comprising nose rectangles similar in style to those of No 4 Squadron, with segments of blue and (Lincoln) green divided by a lightning flash. In the event these were shelved in favour of a 'safer' scheme — blue rectangles outlined in white! Fin markings were composed of the blue lion within a white disc, with the three numerals from the aircraft's serial enlarged to serve as the fin tip code. After disbandment the Flight's three aircraft were used as decoys and in 1975 painted in different experimental camouflage schemes.

Markings — Leuchars TFF
An adaptation of the station crest was applied to the fin, while the three digits of the serial number were repeated in front of the nose roundel, à la No 226 OCU from which some of the aircraft had come. In 1968 these gave way to yellow nose rectangles, each containing a rampant red Scots lion, and thinly in-lined in the same colour — these schemes giving rise to the term by which the TFF was sometimes referred, the 'Royal Scottish Air Force'. The three serial number digits, thus displaced, were moved to the fin tip.

After the migration of No 11 Squadron to Binbrook in 1972 the three TFF Lightnings adopted No 23 Squadron's markings in March that year — XM169 'W', XM144 'X' and XM178 'Y'. XM144 was subsequently preserved and displayed at Leuchars' main gate in its original markings as 'J' of No 74 Squadron.

Markings — Wattisham TFF
Yellow/black/yellow nose bars, thinly outlined in black, remained in vogue throughout this TFF's existence, although fin markings varied from different styles of station crest, to the rear view of a winged cat, which was

Last Leuchars Lightning: F6 XS895 left the base on 30 January 1976 with white and red nose markings (a similar design to the TFF), and blue and white fin marks.
Via Dave Tuplin

Fin detail of XM139 in 1970 showing the new style flash and Wattisham TFF badge.
Author

adopted for a while! There were times when the three Lightnings in use acquired names — 'Korky', 'Jinx' and 'Felix' were among those used.

A single black code letter near the fin tip was discontinued when the cat marking was introduced, and at the same time the flash was moved to the leading edge of the fin. Several of the unit's aircraft carried the Union flag on the fin (as did other Lightning units which visited abroad) and for a while XM139 retained the large numbers '474' appended to the rear fuselage during its participation in the Paris Air Show in 1971.

Right:
The red lions on yellow field (with red trim) of the Leuchars TFF. *Author*

Below:
Wattisham TFF Lightning F1 XM147 'C'. The rectangles are yellow and black.
Geoff Parselle

MAINTENANCE UNITS

The three Maintenance Units mainly concerned with the Lightning were No 33 at Lyneham, which closed in August 1966 when its duties were transferred to No 60 MU at Leconfield. No 60 continued until late in 1976 after which most overhaul, major maintenance and storage work was done at Binbrook. The MU at St Athan was also used, mainly for camouflaging Lightnings, until the early 1980s.

Markings — No 60 MU

In addition to Lightnings 'passing through' the Unit or in store, one or two such aircraft were regularly used as hacks and to provide the resident RAF test pilot with adequate flying practice. Three of these Lightnings carried special No 60 MU markings. The first was XM144, an F1 which was decorated with pale blue rectangles each side of the nose roundel, outlined on upper and lower edges in dark blue, and featuring an orange/red arrow marking running through each segment, and pointing towards the nose of the aircraft. The fin marking was similarly adapted from the Leconfield station crest, and featured a quiver of arrows set within a pale blue disc. XM144 was in use with this décor from at least April until September 1967 when it was succeeded by F6 XR726, which was adorned with the same, unusual decoration until January 1968 when it was delivered to No 5 Squadron.

The third No 60 MU Lightning was F1 XM135, which was used from July 1973 until flown to the Imperial War Museum at Duxford, on 20 November 1974, thereby becoming both the first and the last F1 to be operated by the RAF. It carried the inscription 'FLAG SHIP 60 MU' beneath the cockpit and beneath the pennant and name of Sqn Ldr R. (Bob) W. Turbin, the resident test pilot. It was this aircraft which featured in the much publicised involuntary flight on 22 July 1966 by Wg Cdr 'Taffy' Holden, an engineering officer at No 33 MU, who accidentally engaged reheat while conducting fast taxying engine tests along Lyneham's runway. XM135 needed little persuasion to take off, and the Wing Commander did extremely well to get the aircraft and himself safely back to terra firma after several attempts to land during his 12min flying time, which must have seemed a lifetime!

AKROTIRI STATION FLIGHT

In January 1975 T5 XS452, formerly 'X' of No 56 Squadron, remained at Akrotiri after that unit returned to the UK. Used to give dual check rides for squadrons visiting Akrotiri for APC, it featured a pale pink fin, decorated with a flamingo marking; the spine was also pink, as were the pale blue-outlined nose rectangles. On 21 May 1975 it was ferried to Binbrook.

EMPIRE TEST PILOTS SCHOOL

The ETPS operated the second prototype T4, XL629, with fleet number '23' on its fin, for several years until replacement by T5 XS422 in January 1976. Its wingtips, dorsal spine and fin were painted scarlet, although the fin later reverted to natural metal finish.

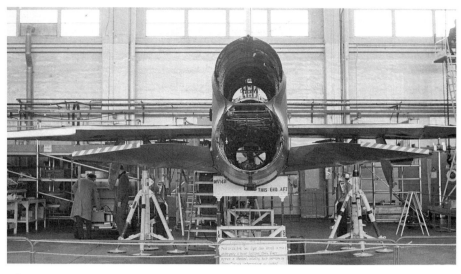

Above:
XN731 'Z', an F2A of No 19 Squadron, undergoes major maintenance including complete re-wiring at No 60 MU, Leconfield, in July 1974. The aircraft already had almost 3,000 flying hours to its credit, and less than two years' service ahead of it before being scrapped. *Author*

Below:
No 56 Squadron Lightning F6 XS921 'Q' is minus almost everything during a major overhaul at No 60 MU, Leconfield, in July 1974. *Author*

Bottom:
Second prototype T4 XL629 is seen as '23' with the Empire Test Pilots School, before retirement when it was 'plinthed' at Boscombe. *ETPS via Flt Lt Smith*

Last to fly Lightnings

Flt Lt Ian Black was the last new pilot to be taught to fly the Lightning, graduating from the LTF when it disbanded in April 1987, to begin a shortened operational tour with No 11 Squadron, itself destined to become the last RAF single-seat air defence fighter squadron within the forseeable future, following its disbandment with Lightnings in the early summer of 1988. Ian is also probably unique in having previously been a navigator on Phantom fighters, and in having a father whose own career in the RAF included the command of two Lightning squadrons.

'Having joined the RAF as a navigator, I always wanted to remain in air defence, and after three years in Germany with a Phantom squadron I decided to apply for my life-long ambition to be a Lightning pilot — nothing else would do! This was a bit of a gamble because at that time, in January 1984, the Lightning's days were numbered and every LTF course was rumoured to be the last. Anyway having worked my way through the training course and TWU I finally got the posting I'd always wanted — 73 Long Course on the LTF. I never considered myself to be a 'natural' pilot but hoped that my previous 700 hours on the F-4 would help me through the radar work, as long as I could fly the aeroplane!

'Rumours were rife in September 1986 that they might cancel our course and I'd go back to the F-4! (The Tornado F3 was at that time still for experienced pilots only.) Taking each day as it came we finally arrived at the Flight at Binbrook for the two weeks of ground school (a welcome break from the four weeks at Valley to fly the Hawk). Having completed the ground school phase someone noticed that at 6ft 2½in I

Below:
Probably the best-kept F6 in the closing months of No 11 Squadron was XR773 'BR', a dark grey bird with pale grey over-wing tanks, photographed returning from detachment at Warton for Tornado F3 trials for BAe. The pilot is Flt Lt Ian Black.
J. Dunnell

AVM George Black (left) with his son, Flt Lt Ian Black, after their momentous flight in Lightning T5 XS452 'BT' of No 11 Squadron on 13 May 1987, just a month after Ian became the last pilot to complete his training on Lightnings. *RAF Binbrook*

might be a bit tall for the Lightning so I was duly kitted up in full winter flying kit and seated unceremoniously in an F3 and measured by the Station Doc; this was the most unnerving part of the course for two reasons: firstly if I didn't fit it would be back to the F-4, and secondly, for the first time I realised that I couldn't see half of the instruments, let alone reach them! Later, with practice, it became far more comfortable, and with this hurdle over it came to the flying phase, and sortie No 1.

'I will never forget my instructor, Flt Lt John Fynes, the Lightning aerobatics pilot for 1987, who was, to say the least, tolerant. If ever you've been on a bicycle going down a steep hill and the brakes fail you'll know how I felt — not the slightest bit in control! Because of the minimal fuel content of the T5 (I always regarded this as an absolute blessing!) sortie lengths were only 25-30min, and there were only five of these prior to going solo. Although the LTF was a 'hard school' the instructors were excellent and more than helpful, so as well as being taught how to be a fighter pilot, I could also make a good pot of tea for six instructors by the end of the course!

'Back to the conversion after the five T5 rides; first solo day had arrived, for which the weather had to be perfect, and unusually for Binbrook, it *was* perfect. The aircraft was F3 XP753 'DA' used by the OC LTF; and it had made its first flight on 16 March 1964. Never again will I have the thrill of sitting at the end of the runway looking over each

shoulder and seeing nobody else, just the two highly-swept wings, then opening up 16,000lb of thrust and climbing steeply into the misty blue sky over the Lincolnshire Wolds — a memory that will stay with me for ever.

'Few people could have thought that when I watched my father display his Lightning at Farnborough in 1962, at the age of two, I'd be flying my first solo 24 years later!

'Compared to the Phantom the Lightning is a delight to fly, with very few vices, but of course being a single-seater the workload is, I believe, more than double, though at the end of the day you do have the satisfaction of having done it all yourself. That apart, I'd still rather go to war in an F-4 if I had to; the Lightning is a fighter pilot's dream, albeit of the 1960s, whereas the F-4 is a flying weapons platform more than capable of its job as an interceptor.'

SEQUEL

On 13 May 1987 Ian Black flew his father in a Lightning T5 of No 11 Squadron, an immensely satisfying achievement for them both. Ian's father, AVM George Black, retired from the RAF shortly afterwards, concluding a distinguished career which began in 1950 when, as a National Serviceman, he trained in Canada before being posted to his 'native' No 612 (County of

Aberdeen) Squadron, RAuxAF, flying Vampire 5s. He subsequently flew Meteor 8s and Hunter 5s with No 263 Squadron at Wattisham before being seconded to No 802 Squadron of the Fleet Air Arm, flying Sea Hawk fighter-bombers during the Suez operations in November 1956. After a tour as an instructor at No 1 FTS flying Vampires, during which he led an aerobatic team named the 'Linton Blacks', he was posted to No 74 Squadron as a Flight Commander in 1960, when he first flew Lightnings. By now a Squadron Leader, George Black's association with Lightnings continued when he was given command of No 111 Squadron in 1964, and led the unit's aerobatic team of F1As then F3s. This was followed by a spell as OC Flying at No 226 OCU during which he exceeded 1,000hr on Lightnings, before once again becoming OC of a front line Lightning unit when he was posted for a tour with No 5 Squadron in 1969.

Neither does the story end there, for the RAF is very much a family business as far as the Blacks are concerned because Ian's brother Stuart was until recently a Squadron Leader navigator flying Tornado F3s with No 229 OCU at Coningsby, and also an artist of considerable talent whose repertoire of railway locomotive subjects has recently been extended to include Lightnings!

Assessing the Legend

When the Lightning entered operational service in 1960 it endowed the RAF with the world's finest supersonic point defence interceptor, and an aircraft which was a quantum leap in performance by comparison with the subsonic Hawker Hunter day fighter and Gloster Javelin all-weather fighter which it gradually supplanted. In terms of fire power, range, endurance, crew comfort and workload, however, the Lightning could still not match the two-seat Javelin FAW8 and 9 which were armed with two or four 30mm Aden cannon plus *four* Firestreak AAMs, and were probably more effective for the designated task of destroying enemy bombers as far out from Britain's shores as possible — at that time a threat posed by the subsonic Soviet 'Badgers', 'Bisons' and 'Bears'.

Soviet supersonic manned bombers were, however, under active development, and could only be effectively countered by a sophisticated supersonic interceptor, which the Lightning typified. So despite the negative and misguided political defence thinking which too often has threatened to become endemic in Britain, the RAF fortuitously found itself possessor of an aircraft which was a generation ahead of its time, thanks to the genius of the design, development and test flying team at English Electric.

The Lightning's initial rate of climb of over 50,000ft/min was outstanding, and remains exceptional even at the conclusion of its operational career, almost 30 years later. Similarly, it has remained the fastest RAF fighter of all time, with acceleration to match its latter-day American counterparts, the much vaunted F-14, F-15, F-16 and F-18, the development of which began only after the Lightning was firmly established in service. The Lightning has always been a pilot's aeroplane — a joy to fly, with an exhilarating performance combined with a demanding workload in terms of weapons system management — which for the élite band of pilots with the ability to 'hack it' provided almost unparalleled flying satisfaction.

Because of its good power-to-weight ratio, excellent flying controls and structural rigidity, the Lightning was more manoeuvrable than its contemporaries, and only found the going hard with the arrival of the new breed of so-called 'agile' fighters, best exemplified by the F-16.

From an operational viewpoint the Lightning was afflicted with that inherent failing of so many previous British fighters — insufficient fuel to remain airborne for any length of time. Although the provision of additional internal tankage in the final F6 version went some way towards remedying the situation, to be fully effective the Lightning was operationally dependant on the availability of air-refuelling tanker support.

Other detrimental features of the Lightning included inadequate armement: its ability to carry only a pair of AAMs supplemented on early and final marks by two 30mm cannon, gave it only half the firepower of either its precursor, the Javelin, or its Phantom and Tornado successors. Similarly, its Airpass radar, though good in its day, was subject to unacceptable 'clutter' from ground and sea returns when the aircraft was flown low-level — as proved the case after 1970 when the main threat swung from high-altitude bombers to very fast low-level strike/attack aircraft.

Although the price for a mint Lightning was under £½ million per copy, no money was subsequently spent on the aircraft; yet an up-date programme to give it new Doppler AI radar, ECM and increased armament in the form of four AIM-9L Sidewinder AAMs would have transformed its latter-day operational efficiency at comparatively little cost. Other desirable improvements were a bubble hood to give better all-round vision, a 'zero-zero' ejection seat, a more modern gunsight, and navigation avionics enhancement.

Nothing could have been done to alleviate the cramped confines of the cockpit nor improve the inaccessibility of its airframe for which the Lightning was infamous among RAF technicians, who developed special skills in extricating components from its tightly packed fuselage 'tube'. It is interesting to note that a complete double engine change on a Lightning could seldom be accomplished in under a week, whereas the same task on its successor, the Tornado F3, takes only about four hours and no chapped knuckles!

However, all these failings pale into insignificance compared with the aircraft's sheer charisma, and the adoration it has attracted from pilots, technicians and an army of Lightning enthusiasts addicted to its sparkling performance and striking silhouette. Unique in so many ways, the Lightning is more than an important part of British aviation history — it has already become a legend.

Individual Aircraft Histories

LIGHTNING F1

WG760 c/n 95001. Prototype P1A. f/f 4.8.54. Handling and performance trials. Fitted with reheat and cambered wing leading edges, later involved in Firestreak trials with A&AEE. Became 7755M on 2.7.62 for ground instructional use, initially at No 8 School of Technical Training, Weeton, then No 4 SoTT St Athan 1965. 71 MU early 66, to RAF Henlow 11.66, initially in pseudo AFDS markings. Aerospace Museum, Cosford, current.

WG765 c/n 95002. Static test airframe only.

WG763 c/n 95003. Second P1A. f/f 18.7.55. Warton. Armament trials A&AEE including detachment to CFE. To Aero Flt RAE Bedford 21.6.57. Allocated 7816M 30.7.63 and transferred to Henlow. Manchester Science & Industry Museum, current.

XA847 c/n 95004. Prototype P1B. f/f 4.4.57. Aerodynamic and reheat trials English Electric and A&AEE. As P1F fitted with large extension to fin, by 5.63 for further aerodynamic tests by EE. 29.4.66 to RAE Farnborough, and grounded for gravel-arrested landing trials. To Henlow 6.69, then exhibited RAF Museum Hendon until 1988.

XA853 c/n 95005. P1B. f/f 5.9.57. Aerodynamic and weapons development trials EE and A&AEE. Withdrawn from use late 1964 and scrapped Warton 2.65.

XA856 c/n 95006. P1B f/f 3.1.58. Structural trials with EE. 24.3.58 to Rolls-Royce, Hucknall, for Avon engine development. Withdrawn from use '67, scrapped '68.

XG307 c/n 95007. First of 20 pre-production aircraft. f/f 3.4.58. Aerodynamic and equipment development by EE until delivery 24.2.64 to 'A' Sqn A&AEE. Withdrawn from use 70, scrapped RAE Bedford 71.

XG308 c/n 95008. f/f 16.5.58. Handling trials with EE until transfer to 'A' Sqn A&AEE by early 1960. Fitted with taller, square-cut F3 type fin at Warton in 1964 for further trials. 29.6.66 to Aero Flt. RAE Bedford. Withdrawn from use 1968 and scrapped.

XG309 c/n 95009. f/f 23.6.58. To 'A' Sqn A&AEE by early 1960 for gun firing trials. To Farnborough late 62 and to Bedford by 64. Returned to Farnborough 12.6.66 and scrapped early 67.

XG310 c/n 95010. f/f 17.7.58. Retained EE for ventral tank jettison and auto ILS trials until transfer to 'A' Sqn A&AEE by early 1960. Converted by EE to F3 prototype, f/f 16.6.62 Warton; aerodynamic and Red Top trials before sustaining damage in landing accident 25.6.64. Used for taxying trials prior to 12.6.68 when dismantled. Fuselage to PEE Foulness.

XG311 c/n 95011. f/f 20.10.58. Retained EE for handling and equipment development until transfer to 'A' Sqn A&AEE by early 60. Shipped from Belfast 7.61 for tropical trials at Khormaksar, Aden, 10.61-11.61. Crashed River Ribble, near Warton, after undercarriage failure 31.7.63.

XG312 c/n 95012. f/f 29.12.58. Retained EE for development work until late 60 then used for AI23 tests by Ferranti. Returned EE (by then BAC) in 1964. Windscreen shattered, final flight 12.10.66. Issued PEE Foulness 22.7.68.

XG313 c/n 95013. f/f 2.59. Employed Firestreak test work by de Havilland and by A&AEE, 4.61 and 5.61 for Microcell 2in rocket trials. BAC to A&AEE 18.6.65. Flown Boscombe Down to Sydenham 25.4.69 and shipped Belfast to Saudi Arabia as G27-115 for use as ground instructional airframe with RSAF at Dhahran. Scrapped 1972.

XG325 c/n 95014. f/f 26.2.59. Retained EE and de Havilland for Firestreak test work. To 'A' Sqn A&AEE by 3.60. With de Havilland again during 1961 for Red Top development. SOC from Ministry of Aviation 23.6.65, airframe issued to 60 MU for store/spare parts. PEE Foulness 7.8.68.

XG326 c/n 95015. f/f 3.59. Retained EE for red oxide fuel trials. To A&AEE by early 61. Returned BAC by 5.64 and stored Warton until 10.67. PEE Foulness 20.9.68.

XG327 c/n 95016. f/f 10.4.59. To 'A' Sqn A&AEE by 3.60 for handling and rocket pod trials. Fitted with F3 fin by Boulton Paul 1961/2. 13.4.66 returned to A&AEE. To BAC Warton late 68. In use RAE Bedford late 69, but withdrawn from use early 70. To 5 SoTT St Athan in 72 as 8188M, more recently to Manston.

XG328 c/n 95017. f/f 18.6.59. Employed EE for equipment and handling tests. To 'A' Sqn A&AEE by early 60. Returned to BAC and fitted with F3 fin 6.65. Last flight 20.1.66 returned BAC by 5.68 for dismantling prior to PEE Foulness.

XG329 c/n 95018. f/f 30.4.59. Retained EE for handling, performance and other trials. Fitted with F3 fin approx 8.64. Noted in overall red paint scheme Warton before delivery to A&AEE where it was used as a chase plane for the TSR2. With de Havilland 6.4.66 to 21.12.66 when returned Boscombe Down. Engineering School, Cranwell 70 and still current.

XG330 c/n 95019. f/f 30.6.59. Retained EE for instrument tests. Fitted with F3 fin; last flight 5.1.65. Used for static OR339 weapons system development 67/68. Withdrawn from use Warton 68. Scrapped.

XG331 c/n 95020. f/f 5.59. Retained EE until transfer de Havilland before delivery A&AEE approx 6.60. Tropical trials Khormaksar, Aden, 11.61-12.61. Fitted with F3 fin and returned to A&AEE. To EE and dismantled 26.6.68. PEE Foulness 4.7.68.

XG332 c/n 95021. f/f 5.59. Retained EE until transfer to de Havilland by 3.61. Crashed on approach to Hatfield 13.9.62 after engine fire.

XG333 c/n 95022. f/f 9.59. Retained EE before use by de Havilland for Firestreak tests. To 'A' Sqn A&AEE by 60. 7.61 shipped from Belfast for tropical trials Khormaksar, Aden, 11.61-12.61. Fitted with F3 fin and re-issued to A&AEE. To BAC Warton by 6.65 and withdrawn from use by 7.68. Scrapped 70.

XG334 c/n 95023. f/f 14.7.59. 23.12.59 to A/AFDS. 5.3.60 crashed off Wells-next-the Sea, Norfolk after hydraulics failure. Wreckage recovered to Warton.

XG335 c/n 95024. f/f 8.59. 12.59 to B/AFDS. 19.2.63 returned Warton, fitted with F3 fin by Boulton Paul. 12.11.62 to A&AEE. 11.1.65 crashed Woodborough, Wiltshire after undercarriage failed to lower.

XG336 c/n 95025. f/f 25.8.59. 12.59 to C/AFDS. Returned to Warton approx 3.62 fitted with F3 fin and delivered to A&AEE for Red Top trials in 9.65. To 1 SoTT Halton as 8091M 6.5.70 for ground instruction. Scrapped 74.

XG337 c/n 95026. f/f 5.9.59. 2.60 to A&AEE. Approx 64 returned Warton, fitted with F3 fin. Reissued A&AEE by 9.66. Red Top trials. BAC Warton by 5.69 target aircraft AI radar trials. Allocated 8056M 3.12.69 and issued 2 SoTT, Cosford, 27.1.70. Later to RAF Cosford Museum.

XM134 c/n 95030. f/f 3.11.59. 31.3.60 to A&AEE. 7.60-10.11.60 lent AFDS. 2.9.63 'A' 74 Sqn 4.64 to 134/226 OCU. 11.9.64 crashed off Happisburgh, Norfolk, after stbd u/c leg failed to lower.

XM135 c/n 95031. f/f 14.11.59. 25.5.60 'D' AFDS. (Lent 74 Sqn as 'R', 7-9.61.) 28.2.63 to 74 Sqn later coded 'B'. 25.7.64 to 135/226 OCU. 12.1.65 to 33 MU, stored; overhauled; and modified for target facilities duties. 22.9.66 to 135/Leuchars TFF. 29.6.71 60 MU (but lent to TFFs). 20.11.74 Duxford Imperial War Museum.

XM136 c/n 95032. f/f 1.12.59. 21.6.60 'E' AFDS. (Lent 74 Sqn as 'S', 7.9.61.) 15.11.62 EE for mods. 1.5.63 to 'C' 74 Sqn. 2.64 to 136/226 OCU. Early 65 to 33 MU for store, overhaul, and target facilities mods. 4.66 to 'B' Wattisham TFF. 12.9.67 crashed Scottow, near Coltishall, after cockpit fire (pilot ejected safely).

XM137 c/n 95033. f/f 14.12.59. 28.6.60 'F' AFDS. (Lent to 74 Sqn as 'T' 7-9.61.) 2.10.62 EE for mods. 3.4.63 to 'D' 74 Sqn. 2.64 to 137/226 OCU. Early 65 to 33 MU for store, overhaul, and target facilities mods. 15.3.66 to 'Y' FCTU, later becoming 'Y' Binbrook TFF. 24.1.68 60 MU overhaul, returning 'Y' Binbrook TFF. Lent Wattisham TFF, suffered Cat 4 damage 7.69 rear fuselage fire. Transported Warton by road 1.10-4.10.69 major repairs. By 8.70 returned 'Y' Binbrook TFF later in year becoming 'Y' 5 Sqn. 18.1.71 60 MU overhaul and store. Lent Wattisham TFF mid 72. 60 MU store by 4.73. 4.11.74 removed store, salvaged 28.11.74, sold for scrap 16.12.74.

XM138 c/n 95034. f/f 23.12.59. 30.6.60 'G' AFDS. 16.12.60 written off after engine fire on Coltishall's runway. Fuselage section used on float 1962 Lord Mayor of London's show.

XM139 c/n 95035. f/f 12.1.60. 2.8.60 to 'C' 74 Sqn. 8.1.63 EE for mods. 21.6.63 to 74 Sqn re-coded 'F'. Spring 64 to 139/226 OCU. Early 65 to 33 MU for store, overhaul and target facilities mods. 4.66 to 139/Leuchars TFF. 24.10.68 Warton, Cat 4 condition resulting from serious fuel pump problems. 19.2.70 'A' Wattisham TFF after repair by BAC. Later uncoded. 31.12.73 stored Wattisham after disbandment of TFF, then decoy.

XM140 c/n 95036. f/f 21.1.60. 2.8.60 'M' 74 Sqn. Approx 6.63 to 60 MU overhaul. 13.8.63 delivery 140/226 OCU. 9.64 lent 111 Sqn then 'R' 111 Sqn by

12.64. Early 65 to 33 MU store. Salvaged 8.66, scrapped 12.66.

XM141 c/n 95037. f/f 9.2.60. 29.8.60 to 'D' 74 Sqn. 16.5.61 Cat 3 damage, rudder detached during formation take-off. Approx 6.63 to 60 MU overhaul. 13.8.63 delivery 141/226 OCU. 20.8.64 33 MU store. Salvaged 8.66, scrapped 12.66 but forward fuselage to Warton via 60 MU.

XM142 c/n 95038. f/f 19.2.60. 30.8.60 to 'B' 74 Sqn. 26.4.63 crashed off Cromer, Norfolk, hydraulic power lost. Pilot ejected safely.

XM143 c/n 95039. f/f 27.2.60. 15.9.60 to 'A' 74 Sqn. Approx 6.63 to 60 MU overhaul. 20.8.63 delivery 143/226 OCU. Early 65 to 33 MU store. 8.66 salvaged, 12.66 scrapped.

XM144 c/n 95040. f/f 14.3.60. 30.9.60 'J' 74 Sqn. 10.12.62 Warton for mods. 24.5.63 returned 74 Sqn and recoded 'G'. 29.9.63 Cat 3 when ventral tank and canopy jettisoned when nose wheel 'up' on landing. 16.6.64 to 144/226 OCU. 17.6.65 33 MU store, overhaul and target facilities mods. 4.7.66 transferred 60 MU as 33 MU closed. 28.1.67 Leconfield Stn Flt/60 MU 'Hack', acquiring 'Golden Arrow' paint scheme by 5.67. 29.12.67 'B' Wattisham TFF, 'Jinx' by 6.69, 'Felix' by 8.69, uncoded by 9.72, to 60 MU 22.9.70 overhaul, 30.7.71 to 144/Leuchars TFF becoming 'X' 23 Sqn early 72 after squadron absorbed TFF last flight 7.11.73, total flying hours 1,564.20. 31.12.73 TFF of 23 Sqn disbanded, aircraft parked airfield as decoy. Refurbished in 79 as 'J' 74 Sqn gate guardian. Current.

XM145 c/n 95041. f/f 18.3.60. A&AEE approx 8.60. 15.1.61 'Q' 74 Sqn. Damaged by fire 61 and returned Warton repair. 14.5.62 to 'Q' 74 Sqn. Recorded 'H' approx 7.63. 2.64 to 145/226 OCU. Early 65 to 33 MU store, overhaul and target facilities mods. 4.66 to 145/Leuchars TFF. 24.1.72 60 MU store. 24.6.74 salvaged, scrapped 12.74.

XM146 c/n 95042. f/f 29.3.60. 4.9.60 'L' 74 Sqn. Approx 6.63 to 60 MU overhaul. 8.63 to 146/226 OCU. 'J' 111 Sqn 12.64-2.65. Early 65 to 33 MU store. 8.66 salvaged, 12.66 scrapped.

XM147 c/n 95043. f/f 7.4.60. 3.9.60 'P' 74 Sqn. Approx 3.63 EE for mods returning approx 6.63 re-coded 'J' 74 Sqn. 2.64 to 147/226 OCU. Lent 111 Sqn 9.64-12.64. Early 65 to 33 MU store, overhaul and mods for target facilities (also at Warton late 65 undercarriage tests following problems earlier in service). 1.7.66 to 'C' Wattisham TFF. 5.69 re-coded 'A' then named 'Felix' and 'Korky' later in year after code removed. 2.4.70 60 MU. 4.2.71 returned Wattisham TFF. Retained base for decoy duty after TFF disbanded 31.12.73.

XM163 c/n 95044. f/f 23.4.60. 4.11.60 'H' AFDS, returned EE, re-delivered AFDS 7.11.60. Lent 74 Sqn as 'Q' 7.61-9.61. 4.9.62 Warton for mods. 3.4.63 'K' 74 Sqn. 2.64 to 163/226 OCU. Early 65 to 33 MU store, overhaul and mods for target facilities duties. 3.66 'A' Wattisham TFF. 5.69 BAC Warton for rebuild returning approx 5.70. 16.2.72 to 60 MU overhaul and store. 6.74 salvaged, scrapped approx 12.74.

XM164 c/n 95045. f/f 13.6.60. 15.7.60 'K' 74 Sqn. 12.11.62 EE Warton for mods. 1.7.63 returned, re-coded 'L' 74 Sqn. 2.64 to 164/226 OCU. Early 65 to 33 MU store, overhaul and mods for target facilities duties. 22.2.66 to 'Z' FCTU, later Binbrook TFF. 17.3.67 canopy off in flight causing Cat 3 damage to fin. 60 MU approx 8.69-early 71, had become 'Z' 5 Sqn, when 5 Sqn temporarily absorbed TFF. 6.7.71 to 'S' Leuchars TFF, later 164/Leuchars TFF. 3.72 60 MU store. 6.74 salvaged, scrapped by 12.74.

XM165 c/n 95046. f/f 30.5.60. 29.6.60 to 'F' 74 Sqn, 60 MU for overhaul approx 6.63. 8.63 to 165/226 OCU. Approx 9.64 to 33 MU store. 8.66 salvaged, scrapped 12.66.

XM166 c/n 95047. f/f 1.7.60. 2.8.60 'G' 74 Sqn. 60 MU overhaul approx 6.63. 30.8.63 to 166/226 OCU. Early 65 to 33 MU store. 8.66 salvaged, scrapped 12.66.

XM167 c/n 95048. f/f 14.7.60. 26.9.60 'H' 74 Sqn. 60 MU overhaul approx 6.63. 9.63 to 226 OCU. '167' by 10.63. Early 65 to 33 MU store. 8.66 salvaged, scrapped 12.66.

XM168 c/n 95049. Static test airframe, never flown.

XM148 and **XM149** never completed.

LIGHTNING F1A

XM169 c/n 95056. f/f 16.8.60. Retained EE various trials including radio and flight refuelling, officially handed to MoA Air Fleet Warton 13.12.60 for test work, during which transferred A&AEE between 8.2.62 and 21.3.62. 14.10.64 to Wattisham where acquired non-standard markings as 'B' 111 Sqn. 8.4.65 to 33 MU. 8.8.66 60 MU store. 13.1.68 'X' Binbrook TFF, markings as 'X' 5 Sqn in spring 71. 29.7.71 60 MU major overhaul and store. 7.9.73 Coltishall 23 Sqn TFF becoming 'W' at Leuchars by 15.9.73. Withdrawn flying duties after disbandment TFFs 31.12.73, used as decoy at Leuchars. Last flight 3.1.74, total hours 811.30.

XM170 c/n 95057. Mercury spillage caused by heavy landing Warton at conclusion of first flight 12.9.60; written-off further flying. Reported total time airborne 14min. Airframe subsequently used for structural and system tests EE, then spare parts before allocation 9 SoTT Newton as 7877M 15.2.65. Fire compound Swinderby by 10.66.

XM171 c/n 95058. f/f 20.9.60. 10.11.60 A&AEE type evaluation and handling tests. 28.11.60 Warton. 28.2.61 'R' 56 Sqn. Recorded 'A' early 3.63. 7.4.65 to 171/226 OCU. 11.9.73 60 MU, salvaged 3.74, scrapped 7.74.

XM172 c/n 95059. f/f 10.10.60. 14.12.60 'S' 56 Sqn. Recorded 'B' early 3.63. To 172/226 OCU approx 3.65. 11.8.65-9.66 to 60 MU major servicing and mods. Again 60 MU 15.10.73-approx 2.74. Withdrawn active 226 OCU use approx 6.74. Stripped of

equipment, displayed Coltishall main gate 24.9.74. Current.

XM173 c/n 95060. f/f 1.11.60. 2.1.61 'V' 56 Sqn. Recoded 'C' approx 3.63. Approx 2.65 to 173/226 OCU. Approx 2.72 to 173/Leuchars TFF. By 6.72 Binbrook TFF (for 11 Sqn), coded '173' approx 10.72. 31.12.73 TFF disbanded. Used Binbrook as decoy, 75 evaluated camouflage. Approx 12.76 Bentley Priory and given 74 Sqn marks!

XM174 c/n 95061. f/f 15.11.60. 15.12.60 'Y' 56 Sqn. Recoded 'D' approx 3.63. 6.6.63 damaged mid-air collision with XM179 'J' but repaired. 19.11.63 landing accident (Cat 4) Wattisham and repaired. 7.7.65 to 174/226 OCU. 19.4.67 damaged by fire when landing, again landing accident Binbrook late summer 68. Lent Leuchars TFF 10.68, transferred to unit by 11.68 becoming 174/ Leuchars TFF. 29.11.68 crashed near Leuchars after fire in the air, pilot ejecting successfully.

XM175 c/n 95062. f/f 23.11.60. 15.12.60 'T' 56 Sqn. Recoded 'E' approx 3.63. Withdrawn active use Wattisham 2.65. To 33 MU store approx 6.65. 60 MU store. 6.4.73 Warton, airframe used static test rig, dismantled and scrapped early 74.

XM176 c/n 95063. f/f 1.12.60. 16.1.61 to 'D' 56 Sqn. Recoded 'F' approx 3.63. Withdrawn active use Wattisham 2.65. 33 MU store approx 6.65. 27.7.66 60 MU store. 29.4.74 removed store, salvaged, scrapped 8.74.

XM177 c/n 95064. f/f 20.12.60. 28.2.61 'N' 56 Sqn. Recoded 'G' approx 3.63. 2.65 to 177/226 OCU. 23.3.66-approx 11.66 60 MU major servicing and mods before returning to 226 OCU. 1.10.69 to 177/Leuchars TFF. 23.4.71 Wattisham TFF. 9.71 to 177/Leuchars TFF becoming 'Y' 23 Sqn (TFF duties)

Below:

Flight refuelling: a Sea Vixen FAW2 of 899 Squadron donates kerosene to No 111 Squadron F1A XM192 'K'. *Flight Refuelling Ltd*

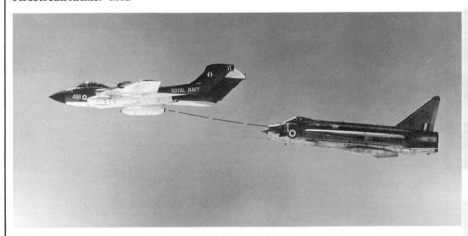

Bottom:

XM216 'P' of 111 Squadron was photographed during high-altitude live firing trials of the 30mm Aden cannon gun pack in the lower fuselage, displacing the usual pair of Firestreak AAMs. *MoD*

by 4.72. 5.72 Wattisham TFF. 14.9.73 to 60 MU. 1.74 salvaged, scrapped by 8.74.

XM178 c/n 96065. f/f 30.12.60. 3.2.61 'O' 56 Sqn. Recoded 'H' approx 3.63. Withdrawn active use Wattisham 3.65. To 33 MU approx 12.5.66 for store, servicing, and mods. 20.6.66 to 178/226 OCU. 22.12.66 60 MU servicing, returning OCU approx 3.67. 3.2.72 to 178/Leuchars TFF becoming 'Y' 23 Sqn (TFF duties) by 5.72. Withdrawn flying after TFFs disbanded 31.12.73, retained at Leuchars as decoy. Last flight 9.1.74, total hours 1,377.45.

XM179 c/n 95066. f/f 4.1.61. 28.2.61 to 'F' 56 Sqn. Recoded 'J' approx 3.63. 6.6.63 destroyed mid-air collision with XM174 'D' practising formation aerobatics, crashed Great Bricett, near Wattisham, pilot injured in ejection.

XM180 c/n 95067. f/f 23.1.61. 8.3.61 'H' 56 Sqn. Recoded 'K' approx 3.63. 2.65 to 180/226 OCU. 60 MU major servicing, repairs and mods 11.65-18.7.66 and 9.1.67-30.3.67. Withdrawn active use 6.74. 10.7.74 Gütersloh decoy, acquiring matt green camouflage later in year.

XM181 c/n 95068. f/f 25.1.61. 3.61 'X' 56 Sqn. EE approx 8.61. 29.9.61 to 'M' 111 Sqn. 3.63 'L' 56 Sqn. Withdrawn active use Wattisham 4.65 before 33 MU by 6.65 for store. 17.8.66 60 MU store. Out of store late 69, brought to current mod state. First flight after four years 8.4.70. 7.5.70 to 'Y' 5 Sqn (TFF), later 'Y' Binbrook TFF. Approx 10.72 coded 181/Binbrook TFF. 31.12.73 withdrawn active use after TFFs disbanded, retained Binbrook as decoy, later to evaluate camouflage. Scrapped.

XM182 c/n 95069. f/f 6.2.61. 13.3.61 'P' 56 Sqn. Recoded 'M' approx 4.63. 2.65 to 182/226 OCU. 60 MU major servicing and mods 21.12.65-3.66, again 11.67-6.68. Lent Binbrook TFF 1-2.73 and 23 Sqn (TFF) 23.7.73-8.73. Withdrawn active use 226 OCU 6.74, flown Gütersloh 10.7.74 decoy purposes, later camouflaged.

XM183 c/n 95070. f/f 9.2.61. 6.3.61 'K' 56 Sqn. 5.5.61 damage after overshooting Wattisham's runway but repaired EE working party. Recoded 'N' approx 3.63. Withdrawn active use Wattisham 3.65, flown 33 MU store. Approx 6.66 to 183/226 OCU. 27.8.70 60 MU. 8.10.71 'X' 5 Sqn (TFF). 60 MU mods approx 6-7.72. Approx 10.72 coded 183/Binbrook TFF. 31.12.73 withdrawn active use after TFFs disbanded, retained as airfield decoy, evaluated camouflage 75. Scrapped.

XM184 c/n 95082. f/f 27.2.61. 13.4.61 'A' 111 Sqn. 1.1.65 to 33 MU servicing and mods. 6.65 to 184/226 OCU. 60 MU major servicing approx 10.66-3.67. 17.4.67 crashed on landing, Coltishall, written-off. Stripped for spares, hulk for fire practice.

XM185 c/n 95083. f/f 28.2.61. 6.3.61 'C' 111 Sqn. 28.6.61 crashed near Wattisham after undercarriage failed to lower. Wreckage 71 MU, one wing later to Henlow.

XM186 c/n 95084. f/f 14.3.61. 13.4.61 'B' 111 Sqn. 18.7.63 crashed Wittering soon after take-off before aerobatic display for NATO VIPs.

XM187 c/n 95085. f/f 20.3.61. 24.4.61 'D' 111 Sqn. 4.64 undercarriage collapsed Wattisham, aircraft relegated ground instructional purposes as 7838 M, issued 9 SoTT Newton. By 78 airframe Coningsby for fire practice.

XM188 c/n 95086. f/f 27.3.61. 30.5.61 'F' 111 Sqn. 18.1.65 to 188/226 OCU. 33 MU major servicing 29.3.65-9.65. 60 MU briefly for servicing 66 while still on OCU strength. 21.6.68 written-off after ran off runway at Coltishall, struck hangar. 4.7.68 SOC, used station fire practice.

XM189 c/n 95087. f/f 30.3.61. 1.5.61 'E' 111 Sqn. 2.65 to 189/226 OCU. 60 MU major servicing 11.66-10.3.67. Withdrawn active OCU service 6.74. 10.7.74 Gütersloh decoy use.

XM190 c/n 95088. f/f 1.5.61. 20.6.61 'G' 111 Sqn. (Flown by Indian AF pilots when India considering purchase of former RAF Lightning F1s.) 6.6.63 Cat 3 damage, subsequently repaired Wattisham EE working party 14.6-30.7.63. 25.2.65 56 Sqn (believed still in 111 marks). 1.4.65 to 190/226 OCU. 15.3.66 crashed North Sea off Cromer after pilot successfully ejected following engine fire.

XM191 c/n 95089. f/f 8.5.61. 28.6.61 'H' 111 Sqn. 9.6.64 written off landing accident Wattisham, aircraft extensively damaged by fire. Nose section display purposes as 7854M, remainder airframe Wattisham's fire compound.

XM192 c/n 95090. f/f 25.5.61. 28.6.61 'K' 111 Sqn. 2.65 to 192/226 OCU. 60 MU major servicing 26.8.65-6.66 then to OCU. 1.10.69 Binbrook TFF (possibly 'Z'). Early 70 Wattisham TFF. 60 MU 10.73 servicing. After TFFs disbanded 31.12.73 redecorated in original scheme as 'K' 111 Sqn, returned Wattisham 27.9.74 display at main gate. Current.

XM213 c/n 95091. f/f 3.6.61. 30.6.61 'L' 111 Sqn. 24.2.65 56 Sqn (believed still in 111 marks). 5.4.65 to 213/226 OCU. 17.6.65 Cat 3 damage Coltishall, repaired on site 60 MU working party, to service 2.8.65. 6.5.66 written off when tail hit runway Coltishall resulting in aborted take-off and crash landing in overshoot area. 11.5.66 SOC.

XM214 c/n 95092. f/f 29.6.61. 1.8.61 'N' 111 Sqn. 1.1.65 33 MU servicing. 4.8.65 to 214/226 OCU. 60 MU major servicing 10.66-4.67. Withdrawn active OCU use by 6.74. 15.6.74 Gütersloh use as decoy.

XM215 c/n 95093. f/f 11.7.61. 2.8.61 'C' 111 Sqn. 2.65 to 215/226 OCU. 60 MU major servicing between 11.66 and at least 3.67. Withdrawn active OCU use by 6.74. 14.6.74 Gütersloh use as decoy.

XM216 c/n 95095. f/f 28.7.61. 29.8.61 to 'P' 111 Sqn. 1.65 to 216/226 OCU 6.65 Cat 4 damage with starter explosion, despatched 22.7.65 road to Warton for repair. 7.9.66 flown Coltishall to rejoin 226 OCU. Withdrawn active OCU use 6.74. 10.7.74 Gütersloh use as decoy.

XM217 and **XM218** Not completed, components as spares.

Below:
Night and all-weather operational flying in the single-seat Lightning placed a very heavy workload on pilots. This illustration of a ground-crewman guiding a No 56 Squadron F1A, XM171 'R', back to its hardstand outside Wattisham's No 3 hangar with the aid of illuminated 'wands', typifies night-flying training sorties. *MoD*

LIGHTNING F2/F2A

XN723 c/n 95096. f/f 11.7.61 EE. 6.2.62 A&AEE. 14.5.62 EE. 2.4.63 Rolls-Royce (Hucknall). 25.3.64 crashed after mid-air fire, Keyham, near Leicester.

XN724 c/n 95094. f/f 11.9.61 EE. 22.5.62 A&AEE. 10.7.62 EE. 5.9.63 33MU 20.10.66 BAC: *F2A*. 18.5.68 'F' 19 Sqn. Withdrawn from use 7.12.76. Allocated 8513M as decoy for Laarbruch.

XN725 c/n 95097. f/f 31.3.62 after modification to F3A standard as systems test aircraft, incorporating Avon 301 engines, fitted with cambered wing. 3.9.63 Filton. 1.4.64 EE, Warton. 5.65 transferred MoA. 30.1.67 RAE Bedford, spell at BAC, Warton 9.10.67-26.4.68. Withdrawn flying by 72, by 8/74 issued PEE Shoeburyness.

XN726 c/n 95098. f/f 29.9.61. 14.2.63 'K' AFDS. .65 33MU 19.10.66 BAC: *F2A*. f/f 28.3.68, 7.6.68 'D'19 Sqn. 2.6.74. Cat 4 lightning strike. 6.72 BAC Warton by road, repaired, f/f 12.3.74. 6.74 'N' 92 Sqn. 4.4.77 RAE Farnborough 23.11.78 PEE.

XN727 c/n 95099. f/f 13.10.61. 25.1.63 'A' 19 Sqn. late 67/early 68 BAC: *F2A*. f/f 25.4.69. 2.2.70 'P' 92 Sqn 8.70 60 MU. 5.11.70 BAC Warton. 2.12.70 'W' 92 Sqn. 4.4.77 RAE Farnborough (8547M). 20.4.78 PEE.

XN728 c/n 95105. f/f 26.10.61. 1.4.63 'B' 92 Sqn. 9.1.68 Cat 4 when failed to get airborne. 3.4.68 BAC Warton in Belfast freighter XR371: *F2A*. 24.6.69 A&AEE. 23.7.69 'F' 92 Sqn. 2.9.70 BAC. 24.11.70 'V' 92 Sqn. 4.4.77 Coningsby (8546M) for decoy. Later scrapped.

XN729 c/n 95106. f/f 3.11.61. 1.3.63 'L' AFDS. 8.64 A&AEE for water-cooled pilots suit and other tropical equipment trials prior to F52. 25.1.67 BAC. f/f as *F52* (G-27-1) 7.3.67. Delivered to Saudi Arabia via Wattisham (9.5.67) and Akrotiri (10.5.67). (See full details under F52 section.)

XN730 c/n 95107. f/f 23.11.61. 12.3.63 'B' 19 Sqn. 4.10.67 BAC: *F2A*. 30.8.68 'J' 92 Sqn. Withdrawn use 7.76. (8496M) decoy, Gutersloh. Deutsches Luftwaffen Museum, Uetersen, W. Germany.

XN731 c/n 95108. f/f 8.1.62. 22.4.63 Handling Sqn Boscombe Down. 6.63 'M' 92 Sqn. 8.66 BAC: *F2A*. f/f 21.3.69. 17.12.69 'L' 92 Sqn. 7.70 BAC, late '70 A&AEE. 11.12.70 'Z' 19 Sqn. Withdrawn 1.77. (8518M) decoy, Laarbruch.

XN732 c/n 95109. f/f 19.1.62. 30.4.63 'H' 92 Sqn. 25.11.68 BAC: *F2A*. 12.8.69 'R' 92 Sqn. Withdrawn 1.77. (8519M) decoy, Laarbruch.

XN733 c/n 95110. f/f 1.2.62. 6.6.63 'L' 92 Sqn. ?/68 Cat 4 starter explosion, by road to BAC. 4.12.68 BAC: *F2A*. 31.12.69 'R' 92 Sqn. 18.6.70 BAC (SBAC Show 9.70). 16.9.70 60 MU. 10.70 'U'/92 Sqn. 2.12.70 'Y' 19 Sqn. Withdrawn 1.77. (8520M) decoy, Laarbruch.

XN734 c/n 95113. f/f 13.7.62 after modification to *F3* standard, with Avon 301s. 1.5.63 MoA. 16.5.63 A&AEE. 31.12.63 EE. 6.12.65 Rolls-Royce. 18.9.67 BAC for conversion *F3A*. 10.69 A&AEE. 5.2.70 60 MU as 8364M. 26.3.73 BAC for Saudi Training School at Warton as G-27-239. 10.12.86 purchased by Aces High Ltd, North Weald, reg as G-BNCA.

XN735 c/n 95114. f/f 23.2.62. 10.5.63 'J' 92 Sqn. 30.8.68 BAC: *F2A*. 25.4.69 'A' 19 Sqn. 1.77 'U' 92 Sqn. (8552M) decoy, Wildenrath by 5.77.

XN767 c/n 95115. f/f 19.2.62. 2.7.63 33 MU. 10.3.66 BAC. 22.7.66 Saudi *F52* 52-655. 26.7.66 delivered RSAF. (See full details under F52 section.)

XN768 c/n 95121. f/f 14.3.62. 5.7.63 33 MU. 6.64 'S' 92 Sqn. Withdrawn use 1973. (8347M) decoy, Gütersloh.

XN769 c/n 95122. f/f 31.3.62. 5.9.63 33 MU. 20.8.65 'F' 92 Sqn. 1.4.68 60 MU. 9.68 'Z' 92 Sqn. 23.12.71 60 MU. Withdrawn from airworthiness condition 1973. London Air Traffic Control Centre RAF West Drayton, on display.

XN770 c/n 95123. f/f 24.4.62. 5.9.62 33 MU. 4.5.66 BAC. 5.5.66. Saudi *F52* 52-656. 11.7.66 delivered to RSAF. (See full details under F52 section.)

XN771 c/n 95124. f/f 29.8.62. 14.11.62 'M' AFDS. 65 33 MU. 21.9.66 BAC: *F2A*. f/f 1.2.68. 21.3.68 'P' 19 Sqn. 1.77 'S' 92 Sqn. 4.4.77 RAE Farnborough. 23.4.78 PEE.

XN772 c/n 95125. f/f 10.5.62. 7.11.63 A&AEE. 7.66 Rolls-Royce. 4.9.67 BAC: *F2A*. 2.8.68 'N' 92 Sqn. 28.1.71 Crashed Diepholz, W. Germany after entering spin at 36,000ft.

XN773 c/n 95126. f/f 13.6.62. 62 A&AEE. 25.5.64 Rolls-Royce. 65 33 MU. 1.10.65 60 MU. 10.7.67 BAC: *F2A*. 26.6.68 'E' 92 Sqn. Withdrawn use early '77 (8521M) decoy, Laarbruch.

XN774 c/n 95127. f/f 27.9.62. 11.62 AFDS. 13.2.63 'C' 19 Sqn. 13.8.69 BAC: *F2A*. f/f 13.4.70. 2.9.70 'F' 92 Sqn. 4.4.77 Coningsby (8551M) decoy.

XN775 c/n 95128. f/f 1.10.62. 17.12.62 'D' 19 Sqn. 7.6.68 BAC: *F2A*. 15.1.69 'B' 92 sqn. Cat 5 9.75 after fuel leaks. (8448M) decoy.

XN776 c/n 95129. f/f 18.10.62. 13.2.63 'E' 19 Sqn. 6.8.64 BAC Warton. 23.9.65 'E' 19 Sqn. 14.1.69 BAC Warton (1,124hr 20min): *F2A*. 13.8.69 'C' 19 Sqn. 1.77 'C' 92 Sqn. 3.3.77 last operational flight (3,294hr 40min). 5.4.77 RAF Leuchars as decoy. Preserved, Museum of Flight, East Fortune, Scotland.

XN777 c/n 95130. f/f 29.10.62. 6.12.62 'N' AFDS. 21.12.62 Cat 4 when entered barrier after 'chute failure, nose u/c leg broken in process. 9.63 reported with 19 Sqn, early 64 use as 'N' AFDS. Later 64 33 MU. 5.10.66 BAC: *F2A*. f/f 2.3.68. 26.3.68 'K' 19 Sqn. 1.77 transferred 92 Sqn as 'K'. Declared non-operational and issued to Wildenrath as decoy (8536M) 6.4.77.

70

Facing page, and Above:
A remarkable sequence showing the failure of the port mainwheel undercarriage to fully retract down on No 92 Squadron F2A XN730 'J' at Gütersloh in September 1971. In Picture A the problem is clearly visible as '730 overflies the base in company with a wingman. Picture B shows the skill of the pilot in landing 'Juliet' on the starboard mainwheel only. Picture C depicts the moment when speed fell off and the port wingtip and defective undercarriage leg came into contact with the runway. In picture D the pilot has deployed his braking parachute to slow down the aircraft as quickly as possible, before coming to a standstill in picture E — quickly surrounded by the emergency crews. XN730 'J' was back in 92 service by 24 August 1972 after repairs to Category 4 damage had been effected. *Via Gunther Kipp*

Below:
'Flagship 92' — XN793 'A', a Lightning F2A of No 92 Squadron photographed in April 1974. *R. L. Ward*

XN778 c/n 95131. f/f 9.11.62. 9.1.63 'F' 19 Sqn. 28.5.64 111 Sqn (on loan). 11.6.64 returned 'F' 19 Sqn. 10.6.68 BAC: *F2A*. f/f 11.12.68. 19.12.68 'H' 19 Sqn. 1.74 transferred 'A' 92 Sqn. 5.4.77 Wildenrath (8537M) as decoy.

XN779 c/n 95132. f/f 20.11.62. 27.3.63 'G' 19 Sqn. 11.3.66 EE, cat 4 with fuel leaks. 3.2.67 'G' 19 Sqn. 9.68 60 MU. 10.68 19 Sqn (possibly coded 'J'). 9.69 60 MU store. 18.2.71 BAC. 13.5.71 60 MU. 8.7.71 'X' 19 Sqn. Withdrawn use 8.73, used for spares (8348 M).

XN780 c/n 95133. f/f 7.12.62. 12.3.63 'H' 19 Sqn. 27.2.68 BAC: *F2A*. 4.10.68 'G' 92 Sqn. 4.3.71 BAC. 23.4.71 'K' 92 Sqn. Withdrawn use 29.9.75 after ground fire at Gütersloh, placed as decoy (8663 M).

XN781 c/n 95134. f/f 12.12.62. 15.3.63 'J' 19 Sqn. 27.1.65 33 MU (350hr 35min). 13.9.66 BAC: *F2A*. 26.2.68 'B' 19 Sqn. 30.12.70 BAC. 2.2.71 'B' 19 Sqn. 1.77 'B' 92 Sqn. 1.4.77 last operational flight (2,768hr 5min). 5.4.77 flown RAF Leuchars decoy duty, as 8538 M.

XN782 c/n 95135. f/f 20.12.62. 19.2.63 'K' 19 Sqn. 27.3.68 BAC: *F2A*. 25.11.68 'H' 92 Sqn. 5.4.77 Wildenrath for decoy duty (8539 M).

XN783 c/n 95136. f/f 26.1.63. 26.3.63 'A' 92 Sqn. 16.11.65 Cat 3 when u/c collapsed. 4.10.68 60 MU. 3.69. 'A' 92 Sqn. 1.5.69 BAC: *F2A*. 11.5.70 'G' 19 Sqn. 11.1.77 Brüggen decoy duty (8526 M).

XN784 c/n 95137. f/f 26.1.63. 19.3.63 'L' 19 Sqn. 30.1.69 BAC: *F2A*. 26.9.69 'G' 19 Sqn. 11.4.70 BAC. 18.6.70 'R' 19 Sqn 1.77 transferred 'R' 92 Sqn. 31.3.77 Brüggen decoy duty (8540 M). Purchased by Air Classik, Munchengladbach, W. Germany 87.

XN785 c/n 95138. f/f 30.1.63. 5.4.63 'C' 92 Sqn. 27.4.64 crashed on approach to disused airfield at Hutton Cranswick, E. Yorks after fuel system problem during air refuelling exercise; pilot did not eject and was killed.

XN786 c/n 95139. f/f 12.2.63. 9.4.63 'D' 92 Sqn. 29.10.68 BAC: *F2A*. 1.7.69 'M' 19 Sqn. 4.8.76 badly damaged in ground fire, Gütersloh. (8500 M) decoy.

XN787 c/n 95140. f/f 15.2.63. 22.3.63 'M' 19 Sqn. 1.7.69. BAC: *F2A*. 20.5.70 'L' 92 Sqn. 31.12.76 Laarbruch for decoy duties (8522 M).

XN788 c/n 95141. f/f 25.2.63. 23.5.63 Pool aircraft Leconfield, used 'R'/92 Sqn. 25.5.64 111 Sqn (loan). 3.7.64 'R' 92 Sqn. 12.8.69 BAC: *F2A*. 5.7.70 'P' 92 Sqn. 31.3.77 Brüggen decoy duties (8543 M).

XN789 c/n 95142. f/f 11.3.63. 26.4.63 'G' 92 Sqn. 8.66 33 MU. 5.9.66 BAC: *F2A*. f/f 12.10.67. 15.1.68 Handling Sqn, Boscombe Down. 68 60 MU. 23.1.69 'C' 19 Sqn. Recoded 'J' 19 Sqn by 2.70 11.1.77 Brüggen decoy duty (8527 M).

XN790 c/n 95143. f/f 20.3.63. 25.4.63 'E' 92 Sqn, then 'K' 92 Sqn. 26.6.68 BAC: *F2A*. 30.1.69 'L' 19 Sqn. 31.12.76 Laarbruch decoy duty (8523 M).

XN791 c/n 95144. f/f 4.4.63. 9.5.63 'P' 19 Sqn. 21.3.68 BAC: *F2A*. f/f 8.10.68. 29.10.68 'D' 92 Sqn. 12.1.77 Brüggen decoy duty (8524 M).

XN792 c/n 95145. f/f 19.4.63. 24.6.63 'N' 92 Sqn. 2.8.68 BAC: *F2A*. 21.3.69 'M' 92 Sqn. 12.1.77 Brüggen decoy duty (8525 M).

XN793 c/n 95146. f/f 1.5.63. 21.6.63 'K' 92 Sqn. 26.9.68 BAC: *F2A*. 1.5.69 'A' 92 Sqn. 6.74 'H' 19 Sqn 1.77 'X' 92 Sqn. 6.4.77 Wildenrath decoy duty (8544 M).

XN794 c/n 95147. f/f 16.5.63. 5.9.63 33 MU. 29.10.65 'P' 92 Sqn. 5.67 'W' 19 Sqn. Withdrawn 73. Decoy at Gütersloh (8349 M).

XN795 c/n 95148. f/f 30.5.63. 13.7.63 33 MU, 7.7.64 MoA. 9.7.64 BAC: *F2A*. 21.12.67 Min Tech. 12.11.68 A&AEE. 4.77 Bedford (RAE), fitted with 27mm Mauser cannon for Tornado trials, then 'chase' aircraft at Warton.

XN796 c/n 95149. f/f 12.7.63. 11.10.63 33 MU. 29.4.66 BAC. 8.7.66 became *F52* 52-657. Written off on take-off 20.9.66 replaced by XN729 in 5.67.

XN797 c/n 95150. f/f 5.9.63. 4.10.63 33 MU. 29.4.66 BAC. 22.7.66 became *F52* 52-658, delivered to RSAF. (For full details see under F52 section.)

LIGHTNING F3

XP693 c/n 95116. f/f 16.6.62. Salmesbury-Warton, without ventral tank (usual configuration for most Lightning F1/2/3/4 initial flights) by J. L. Dell. Retained EE development work including radio/radar cooling trials. 24.5.63 A&AEE for F3 clearance. 14.10.63 Warton for trials. 1.66 A&AEE trials. 1.67 conv to F3A (Interim F6) standard at Warton. For full details see under F6.

XP694 c/n 95117. f/f 1.5.63. Retained Warton for trials. 1.8.63 A&AEE. Used in AI23B development. 4.65 to full F3 standard. 26.1.67 60 MU. 18.5.67 'D' 29 Sqn. After 29 Sqn disbanded late 74 retained Wattisham until 1.75 when issued as 'V' 56 Sqn. 26.7.76 Binbrook, becoming 'A' LTF. 8.77 store. 2.78 final RAF 'silver' Lightning to receive green/grey camouflage. 2.78 'R' 5 Sqn. Painted as 'R' 29 Sqn for 25th anniversary 8.79. 1.3.82 'A' LTF. By 13.7.82 'BO' 11 Sqn. 21.11.84 stored. Scrapped late 87.

XP695 c/n 95119. f/f 20.6.63. Retained EE. 1.1.64 'R' AFDS. 31.1.66 'R' FCTU. 3.7.66 BAC Warton mod to full F3 standard (440 flights, 321hr). 26.7.67 A&AEE. 4.10.68 60 MU. 3.1.69 'N' 56 Sqn. 14.10.71 'L' 29 Sqn. 9.72 'L' 111 Sqn. 8.73 60 MU. 5.74 'O' 11 Sqn. 12.77 'M' 11 Sqn. 9.80 store. 6.82 LAF. 4.83 'BM' 11 Sqn. 15.3.84 Decoy as 8808M. 10.11.86 Burnt/destroyed.

XP696 c/n 95120. f/f 2.6.63. Retained by EE. 14.1.64 'S' AFDS. 31.1.66 'S' FCTU. 15.2.66 A&AEE, Red Top trials. 5.6.67 60 MU. 27.7.67 BAC mod to full F3. 3.6.69 60 MU. 26.7.70 '696' 226 OCU. White fin/spine for 74 aeros display champion Flt Lt Peter Chapman. 8.74 Binbrook. 10.74 LCU Wattisham, reduced to spares. 10.75 PEE Shoeburyness.

XP697 c/n 95151. f/f 18.7.63. 13.8.63 Filton on second flight for conv to F3A (Interim F6). For full details see under F6.

XP698 c/n 95152. f/f 28.8.63. 12.63 A&AEE. 7.64 BAC mod to full F3. 19.9.64 'F' 74 Sqn. 11.66 BAC. 1.67 'T' 56 Sqn. 10.6.67 'B' 29 Sqn. 16.2.72 collided in night exercise, North Sea, with XP747 (also crashed) 40 miles E of Ipswich (1,360hr).

XP699 c/n 95153. f/f 2.9.63. 10.4.64 A&AEE. 6.64 Wheelus AFB Libya for F3 tropical trials, then Warton for refurbishment. 30.11.64 33 MU. 23.2.66 'O' 56 Sqn. 3.3.67 crashed nr Finchingfield, Essex, while overshooting RAF Wethersfield, after fuel feed problem, which caused fuel fire (299.30hr).

XP700 c/n 95154. f/f 6.6.63. 14.4.64 'A' 74 Sqn. 4.66 Warton for possible conv to F6 (not undertaken). 8.66 Wattisham store. 11.66 'P' 56 Sqn. 17.4.67 'Z' 111 Sqn. 22.6.67 60 MU. 5.68 'K' 29 Sqn. 7.8.72 crashed Gt Waldingfield, Suffolk, following engine fire caused by tail bumper striking runway and rupturing ventral tank; pilot ejected safely (1,653.15hr).

XP701 c/n 95155. f/f 14.9.63. 7.7.74 A&AEE and Warton for misc trials until 8.67 'M' 29 Sqn. 9.70 'M' 111 Sqn. 2.72 'F' 29 Sqn. 11.74 stored Wattisham. 13.5.75 'W' 56 Sqn. 28.6.76 Binbrook store. 2.78 'O' 11 Sqn. 13.1.81 'BN' 11 Sqn. 5.84 'AN' 5 Sqn. 25.2.85 'AR' 5 Sqn. 4.87 allocated 8924M after 13 months' storage. 7.9.87 Decoy, scrapped late 87.

XP702 c/n 95156. f/f 19.9.63. 14.5.64 'C' 74 Sqn. 1.10.66 BAC. 11.66 'R' 56 Sqn. 13.8.71 60 MU store. 1.74 'C' 29 Sqn. 1.75 'W' 56 Sqn. 5.75 'U' 56 Sqn. 28.6.76 stored Wattisham, then 60 MU. 9.77 Binbrook store. 6.79 11 Sqn and LTF on loan. 26.6.79 'P' 5 Sqn. 10.79 'N' 11 Sqn. 4.81 'BO' 11 Sqn. 7.8.82 St Athan respray in light grey, returning 28.8.82 to LAF. Stored. Scrapped late 87.

XP703 c/n 95157. f/f 28.9.63. 8.6.64 'G' 74 Sqn. 10.66 Wattisham. 12.66 'S' 56 Sqn. 29.8.71 60 MU store. 11.8.72 'G' 29 Sqn. 4.2.75 60 MU. 23.5.75 BAC Warton for stressing/structural tests having completed 3,000 flying hours. Retained for structural testing up to 3,500hr. Scrapped by 6.76.

XP704 c/n 95158. f/f 17.10.63. 15.6.64 'H' 74 Sqn. 28.8.64 crashed Leuchars after spinning into ground during practice aerobatic display (36.40hr).

XP705 c/n 95159. f/f 12.10.63. 26.6.64 'K' 74 Sqn. 12.66 Wattisham. 2.67 'W' 56 Sqn. 1.3.67 'K' 29 Sqn. 6.67 coded '90' for Paris Salon. 5.68 'B' 29 Sqn. 6.69 'Z' 111 Sqn. 7.69 'L' 29 Sqn. 8.7.71 crashed in Mediterranean off Akrotiri following jet pipe fire (1,854hr).

XP706 c/n 95160. f/f 28.10.63. 13.6.64 'L' 74 Sqn. 9.66 60 MU. 12.66 'D' 111 Sqn. 1.70 'F' 111 Sqn. 6.74 'R' 23 Sqn. 3.11.75 Binbrook. 12.75 LTF. 11.76 store. 8.79 'R' 5 Sqn. 1.82 store. 7.9.82 'BM' 11 Sqn. 1.7.83 'DD' LTF. 2.86 stored. 4.87 allocated 8925M. 9.87 Decoy. Scrapped late 87.

XP707 c/n 95161. f/f 13.11.63. 18.8.64 'A' 23 Sqn. 8.67 'H' 29 Sqn. 10.70 'F' 29 Sqn. 6.9.74 BAC Filton for refurbishment and store. 5.75 Wattisham. 26.7.76 5 Sqn. 1.77 'P' 5 Sqn. 18.1.78 mothballed. 5.80 LTF loan. 22.9.80 'BM' 11 Sqn. 6.81 'BG' 11 Sqn. 8.81 'BM' 11 Sqn. 1.86 'BO' 11 Sqn after store. 5.86 'DB' LTF. 19.3.87 crashed near Binbrook during practice aeros display when engine flamed out in negative G turn, at 5,000ft.

XP708 c/n 95162. f/f 20.11.63. 18.8.64 'B' 23 Sqn. 8.67 'F' 29 Sqn. 2.68 60 MU. Late 69 'N' 29 Sqn. 4.2.75 60 MU store. 9.1.76 scrapped.

XP735 c/n 95163. f/f 4.12.63. 16.9.64 'E' 23 Sqn. 5.67 approx 'L' 29 Sqn. 30.1.69 60 MU. 7.69 'J' 29 Sqn. 13.5.74 Cat 3R at Coltishall following brake failure, went into crash barrier (1,992.40hr). Repaired on site, 9.1.75 60 MU. 6.75 salvaged and scrapped.

XP736 c/n 95164. f/f 13.12.63. 17.9.64 'F' 23 Sqn. 22.9.67 60 MU store. 2.4.69 'G' 29 Sqn. 22.9.71 crashed 30 miles off Lowestoft (1,510hr).

XP737 c/n 95165. f/f 1.1.64. 21.10.64 'L' 23 Sqn. 16.9.67 'J' 29 Sqn. 5.71 '737' 226 OCU. 5.9.74 Filton for refurbishment. 10.74 Wattisham store. 10.75 Struck off charge Cat 5C. Stripped by Engineering Wing, but then subsequently re-built. 18.5.76 60 MU. 7.76 'P' 11 Sqn. 26.7.78 'N' 11 Sqn. 17.8.79 crashed Irish Sea, off Valley, after port u/c failed to lower.

XP738 c/n 95166. f/f 18.1.64. 4.11.64 33 MU. 7.11.64 'G' 111 Sqn. 9.8.68 60 MU. 2.4.69 'E' 111 Sqn. 10.12.73 wheels-up landing at Wattisham resulted in damage beyond economic repair. Stripped for spares 6.74.

XP739 c/n 95167. f/f 20.1.64. 12.11.64 33 MU. 15.1.65 'H' 111 Sqn. 29.9.65 crashed on approach to Wattisham, near Stowmarket, after double flame-out.

XP740 c/n 95168. f/f 1.2.64. 30.12.64 'J' 111 Sqn.

Below:

Killing ground, Wattisham, May 1975, when many former Nos 29 and 111 Squadron Lightning F3s were prematurely scrapped after worthwhile components had been salvaged to keep flying those still in service. *Martin Horseman*

1.70 rear fuselage fire at Binbrook, 60 MU for repairs. 7.70 '740' 226 OCU. 12.70 60 MU. 2.71 'B' 111 Sqn. 30.9.74 Wattisham store. 19.4.75 dumped after being SOC. 10.75 PEE Shoeburyness.

XP741 c/n 95169. f/f 4.2.64. 22.12.64 'K' 111 Sqn. 30.7.70 60 MU. 20.5.71 'D' 111 Sqn. 2.10.74 Binbrook. 30.10.74 'X' 5 Sqn. 7.2.75 'N' 11 Sqn. 11.3.76 store then 60 MU before returning as 'N' 11 Sqn. 7.78 store. 7.80 'O' 11 Sqn. 11.80 'BO' 11 Sqn. 4.81 'DD' LTF. 4.83 'AQ' 5 Sqn then stored, and used for spares until 7.86 when restored to flying condition. 3.2.87 'DA' LTF. 30.4.87 'AR' 5 Sqn as 1987 aerobatic aircraft. 30.9.87 Manston fire practice.

XP742 c/n 95170. f/f 12.2.64. 10.2.65 'L' 111 Sqn. 27.7.68 60 MU. 8.68 'G' 111 Sqn. 7.5.70 crashed, North Sea, after reheat fire (1,258hr).

XP743 c/n 95171. f/f 18.2.64. 18.2.64 33 MU. 4.65 'G' 56 Sqn. 7.1.69 60 MU. 11.69 returned 56 Sqn. 9.11.71 60 MU. 21.8.72 'B' 29 Sqn. 12.74 Wattisham store. 9.1.75 60 MU store and disposal. 29.1.75 SOC and sold for scrap.

XP744 c/n 95172. f/f 25.2.64. 9.3.65 33 MU. 22.4.65 'H' 56 Sqn. 28.3.68 60 MU. 3.1.69 'G' 56 Sqn via Wattisham. 11.5.71 crashed eight miles southeast of Akrotiri after fire warning (1,304.45hr).

XP745 c/n 95173. f/f 18.3.64. Early 65 33 MU. 20.5.65 'J' 56 Sqn. 8.69 60 MU. 17.8.69 'H' 29 Sqn. 12.74 Wattisham store. 4.2.75 60 MU for salvage, reprieved, allocated 8453M. 14.12.76 RAF Boulmer as H/29 as gate guardian.

XP746 c/n 95174. f/f 26.3.64. 3.65 33 MU. 15.4.65 'K' 56 Sqn. 12.11.69 60 MU. 4.8.70 'J' 111 Sqn. 10.74 Wattisham store. 4.75 SOC. 10.76 PEE Shoeburyness.

XP747 c/n 95175. f/f 8.5.64. Early 65 33 MU. 25.6.65 'L' 56 Sqn. 11.5.66 Cat 4R damage after port main u/c broke when a/c ran off Wattisham runway. Repaired by 60 MU. 11.69 60 MU. 22.7.69 29 Sqn, later coded 'S' 29 Sqn. 16.2.72 collided with XP698 at night over North Sea (1,320hr).

XP748 c/n 95176. f/f 4.5.64. 33 MU early 65. 6.65 Warton. 4.8.65 'M' 56 Sqn. 8.69 60 MU. 5.5.70 'G' 111 Sqn. 3.11.72 'P' 11 Sqn. 20.12.74 Binbrook store. 19.5.75 allocated 8446M. 29.5.77 mounted on plinth at Binbrook gate in both 5 and 11 Sqn marks. Scrapped late summer 88.

XP749 c/n 95177. f/f 11.12.63. 8.4.64 'T' AFDS. 22.12.65 'B' 111 Sqn. 8.69 60 MU. 27.10.70 'K' 111 Sqn. 10.74 Wattisham store. 26.3.76 Binbrook. 30.8.77 'A' LTF. 9.79 store. 12.81 'DB' LTF. 29.2.84 St Athan, returning 6.4.84 in dark grey scheme. 4.84 'BK.1' 11 Sqn. 5.84 recoded 'BK.2' 11 Sqn. 4.85 'BO' 11 Sqn. 11.85 'DB' LTF. 19.5.86 'DA' LTF. 10.86 store. 15.5.87 allocated 8926M. 8.87 Decoy; scrapped late 87.

XP750 c/n 95178. f/f 3.1.64. 1.6.64 'U' AFDS. 23.12.65 'H' 111 Sqn. 17.2.66 Lent 56 Sqn. 1.2.68 60 MU; returning as 'H' 111 Sqn 9.68, again at 60 MU 7.73-23.12.73. 15.5.74 'P' 23 Sqn. 20.10.75 Binbrook. 4.76 LTF, becoming 'B'. 2.79 store. 2.80 LAF. 19.2.80 'Q' 5 Sqn. 10.80 'AQ' 5 Sqn. 7.82 store. 23.2.84 'DE' LTF. 2.85 store. 4.85 allocated 8927M. 9.87 Decoy, and scrapped.

XP751 c/n 95179. f/f 16.3.64. 29.4.64 'B' 74 Sqn. 10.66 Wattisham. 2.11.66 'K' 23 Sqn. After spells at 60 MU 67/68, by 18.5.68 to 'L' 111 Sqn. 15.5.74 'Q' 23 Sqn. 31.10.75 Wattisham store. 3.11.75 Binbrok store. 11.11.75 LTF, coded 'C' LTF by 10.76. 12.11.76 Cat 3 landing accident caused withdrawal until 12.7.78. 9.78 'S' 5 Sqn. 10.80 store. 7.82 'AQ' 5 Sqn. 22.11.84 'DB' LTF. 9.86 'DA' LTF. 10.86 landed with rear fuselage fire, stored. 3.87 allocated 8928M. 9.87 Decoy, scrapped late 87.

XP752 c/n 95180. f/f 20.4.64. 1.6.64 'D' 74 Sqn. 10.66 Wattisham store. 2.67 'O' 23 Sqn. 8.67 'Y' 111 Sqn. 3.3.69 60 MU. 1.70 'D' 111 Sqn. 20.5.71 mid-air collision with French AF Mirage IIIe over Colmar. Both a/c landed safely, but intake duct severely damaged, and a/c withdrawn from use as 8166M after return of wreck to Coltishall.

XP753 c/n 95181. f/f 8.5.64. 23.6.64 'J' 74 Sqn. 9.66 Wattisham store. 2.67 'Y' 111 Sqn. 13.7.67 60 MU. 26.3.68 'C' 56 Sqn; by 8.71 'J' 56 Sqn. 9.11.71 60 MU. 19.11.73 Binbrook, 12.73 'Y' 11 Sqn. 15.1.74 'O' 11 Sqn. 2.74 'L' 11 Sqn, then 'X' 11 Sqn. 11.4.74 'X' 5 Sqn. 10.74 store. 2.75 'Q' 11 Sqn. 5.75 'X' 5 Sqn. 6.76 'Q' 5 Sqn. By 2.77 'S' 5 Sqn. By 7.81 'DC' LTF after storage since 10.80. 28.3.83 St Athan, returning 15.4.83 in two-tone dark/medium grey scheme. 'DC' LTF used as 83 aeros a/c by Flt Lt M. Thompson, who was killed on 26.8.83 when a/c crashed off Scarborough beach while en route Teesside.

XP754 c/n 95182. f/f 5.6.64. 31.7.64 'M' 74 Sqn. 9.66 Wattisham. 1.67 'X' 5 Sqn. 2.67 'X' 111 Sqn. Between 18/29.9.67 re-coded 'A' 111 Sqn. By 18.3.68 'H' 111 Sqn. 13.6.68 60 MU. 9.68 'R' 111 Sqn. 30.9.74 SOC and scrapped.

XP755 c/n 95183. f/f 15.6.64. 31.7.64 'P' 74 Sqn. 11.66 Wattisham. 2.67 'U' 56 Sqn. 3.7.70 60 MU. 29.6.71 'E' 29 Sqn. 12.74 Wattisham store. 2.75 60 MU for disposal. 25.6.75 SOC and scrapped.

XP756 c/n 95184. f/f 22.6.64. 24.8.64 'C' 23 Sqn. 8.67 Wattisham becoming 'K' 29 Sqn. 27.5.68 60 MU. 8.69 'E' 29 Sqn. 7.4.70 Cat 4 after engine fire, repaired on site by 60 MU by 7.70. 25.1.71 crashed off Yarmouth after reheat fire (1,149.15hr).

XP757 c/n 95185. f/f 4.7.64. 25.9.64 'G' 23 Sqn. 19.9.67 60 MU. 7.12.67 'F' 29 Sqn. 9.7.70 60 MU. 16.3.71 'M' 29 Sqn. 12.74 Wattisham store. 9.1.75 60 MU for disposal. 6.75 SOC and scrapped.

XP758 c/n 95186. f/f 10.7.64. 'D' 23 Sqn. 1.11.67 Wattisham store. 5.1.68 60 MU. 17.5.68 'S' 111 Sqn. 3.4.74 'S' 29 Sqn. 12.74 Wattisham store. 18.2.75 60 MU. 6.75 SOC and scrapped.

XP759 c/n 95187. f/f 14.8.64. 1.10.64 'J' 23 Sqn (6.67 Paris Salon, coded '116'). Late 67 to 60 MU. 28.3.68 'T' 56 Sqn, by 1.70 'C' 56 Sqn. 29.2.72 60 MU. 4.5.73 'S' 29 Sqn. 29.8.73 damaged by engine fire in flight, but repaired (1,846.55hr). 10.73 'G' 111 Sqn. 15.5.74 'R' 23 Sqn. 8.74 'F' 111 Sqn. 10.74 Wattisham store. 4.75 SOC and scrapped, parts to Binbrook.

XP760 c/n 95188. f/f 26.8.64. 15.10.64 'K' 23 Sqn. 24.8.66 crashed, North Sea, off Seahouses, Northumberland (428.5hr).

XP761 c/n 95189. f/f 26.8.64. 27.10.64 'N' 23 Sqn. 10.67 'Z' 111 Sqn. 16.9.72 'O' 11 Sqn. 25.7.74 'Q' 11 Sqn. 14.10.74 last flight, when time expired. Allocated 8438M and issued to Lightning Servicing School, Binbrook, until 82 when used as decoy. 10.11.86 burnt.

XP762 c/n 95190. f/f 3.9.64. 26.1.65 'M' 111 Sqn. 3.69 60 MU. 11.69 'C' 111 Sqn. 7.74 noted as 'D' 111 Sqn, by 8.8.74 reverted to 'C' 111 Sqn. 9.74 'A' 29 Sqn. 9.1.75 60 MU for disposal. 25.6.75 SOC and scrapped.

XP763 c/n 95191. f/f 11.9.64. 27.10.64 'M' 23 Sqn. 7.66 60 MU. Early 67 'K' 56 Sqn. 10.67 'G' 29 Sqn. 29.9.68 60 MU. 15.3.69 'P' 29 Sqn. 12.74 Wattisham store. 3.75 SOC and scrapped.

XP764 c/n 95192. f/f 19.9.64. 3.11.64 'H' 74 Sqn. 2.6.66 Wattisham overhaul (BAC). Early 67 'V' 56 Sqn. 5.67 'V' 23 Sqn. 6.67 60 MU. 7.67 'E' 29 Sqn. 8.69 60 MU. 9.69 'C' 29 Sqn. 30.10.72 'S' 5 Sqn. 30.10.74 Binbrook store. 2.3.77 'O' 11 Sqn. 26.5.79 'B' LTF. 23.10.80 'DB' LTF. 17.11.81 'AR' 5 Sqn. 22.1.85 St Athan. 3.3.85 returned in dark grey scheme. 21.3.86 'DC' LTF. 4.87 allocated 8929M. By 7.9.87 decoy; scrapped late 87.

XP765 c/n 95193. f/f 26.9.64. 27.11.64 33 MU store. 6.9.65 'N' 56 Sqn. Later in month displayed at 'Unison 65' at RAF Cranwell fitted with dummy overwing tanks. Late 4.67 'A' 29 Sqn. 16.3.70 60 MU. 24.9.70 'A' 29 Sqn. 12.74 Wattisham store. 4.75 SOC and scrapped.

XR711 c/n 95194. f/f 6.10.64. 2.12.64 'A' 111 Sqn. 24.8.67 60 MU. 4.3.68 'A' 111 Sqn. 29.10.71 crashed Wattisham after failing to get airborne following reheat fire during take-off. Airframe cannibalised for spares (1,667.25hr).

XR712 c/n 95195. f/f 12.10.64. 19.11.64 33 MU. 18.1.65 'B' 111 Sqn. 26.6.65 crashed after shedding pieces of tailpipe during Exeter Air Show at Mach 0.7; pilot tried emergency diversion to RAF St Mawgan but crashed near Padstow, Cornwall, having successfully ejected (145hr).

XR713 c/n 95196. f/f 21.10.64. 8.1.65 'C' 111 Sqn. 10.69 60 MU. 6.70 'B' 111 Sqn. 9.2.71 60 MU. 25.11.71 'A' 111 Sqn. 29.8.74 Binbrook. 31.10.74 'S' 5 Sqn. 3.76 LTF. 8.78 'C' LTF. 10.78 'O' 11 Sqn. 7.80 store. 5.5.82 'AR' 5 Sqn. Store 10.4.83-8.85. 9.85 'DD' LTF. 31.10.85 'DC' LTF. 5.3.87 Lossiemouth. 11.3.87 Leuchars. Allocated 8935M, restored as 'C' 111 Sqn c65 for display purposes at 111 Sqn HQ. Current.

XR714 c/n 95197. f/f 3.11.64. 8.1.65 'D' 111 Sqn. 27.9.66 crashed on Akrotiri runway after being caught in jet blast during formation take-off. 16.11.67 SOC.

XR715 c/n 95198. f/f 14.11.64. 8.1.65 'E' 111 Sqn. 17.4.69 60 MU. By 1.7.70 'R' 29 Sqn. 13.2.74 crashed Blyford Green, Suffolk.

XR716 c/n 95199. f/f 19.11.64. 4.2.65 'F' 111 Sqn. 12.69 60 MU. 7.70 '716' 226 OCU. 11.9.74 'U' 29 Sqn. 12.74 Wattisham store. 30.1.75 'U' 56 Sqn. 26.11.75 LTF. 8.77 'C' LTF. 20.10.80 'AS' 5 Sqn. 15.2.83 store. 5.3.87 air tested as 'DE' LTF but transferred 'AQ' 5 Sqn by 29.4.87 for aeros display a/c. 30.9.87 Cottesmore for battle damage repair.

XR717 c/n 95200. f/f 25.11.64. 26.3.65 'B' 56 Sqn. 14.1.69 60 MU. 10.70 'B' 56 Sqn. 11.71 60 MU. 29.3.72 A&AEE. 8.74 stored, Boscombe Down. 9.74 Scrapped.

XR718 c/n 95201. f/f 14.12.64. 1.4.65 'C' 56 Sqn. 1.5.67 'C' 29 Sqn. 9.69 60 MU. 5.70 '718' 226 OCU. 3.9.74 BAC Filton for refurbishment and sales demo pending disposal. 10.74 Wattisham store. 10.75 Stripped for spares and moved to fire dump, then retrieved and rebuilt! 2.6.76 60 MU. 21.6.76 'S' 5 Sqn. 12.76 'C' LTF. 4.77 store. 18.1.78 'P' 5 Sqn. 2.79 'B' LTF. 5.79 store. 22.6.79 'C' LTF. 11.7.79 store. 25.3.80 'C' then 'DC' LTF. 4.81 store. 2.83 'AS' 5 Sqn. 6.83 store. 30.3.84 St Athan for respray in dark grey scheme, returning 8.5.84. Early 5.84 'BK1' 11 Sqn, re-coded 'BK2' 11 Sqn by 30.5.84. 11.84 store. 29.10.85 'DB' LTF. 11.85 store. 23.12.85 11 Sqn. 15.4.86 'DE' LTF. 30.10.86 'DA' LTF. 1.87 store. 3.87 allocated 89342M and issued Wattisham for battle damage repair.

XR719 c/n 95202. f/f 18.12.64. 16.4.65 'D' 56 Sqn. 9.68 60 MU. 16.4.69 'D' 56 Sqn. 9.11.71 60 MU. 12.71 '719' 226 OCU. 7.6.73 crashed Coltishall and SOC.

XR720 c/n 95203. f/f 24.12.64. 29.3.65 33 MU. 8.4.65 'E' 56 Sqn. 9.68 60 MU. 14.7.69 'E' 56 Sqn. 5.10.71 60 MU. 8.10.71 'L' 29 Sqn. 13.10.71 60 MU store. 8.2.73 'M' 11 Sqn. 16.2.76 LTF. 26.3.76 'M' 11 Sqn. 9.12.77 store. 29.4.81 'DC' LTF. 11.2.82 'BN' 11 Sqn. 16.9.82 'DA' LTF. 2.85 store. 4.87 allocated 8930M. 9.87 Decoy, scrapped late 87.

XR721 c/n 95204. f/f 5.1.65. 8.4.65 'F' 56 Sqn. 5.1.66 crashed during practice diversion to RAF Bentwaters, at Helingham, when No 1 engine flamed out. Canopy fault prevented ejection; pilot killed in ensuing crash (220.50hr).

XR722 c/n 95205. f/f 23.1.65. Retained Warton for conversion to first F53.

XR748 c/n 95213. f/f 13.4.65. Retained BAC. 21.8.67 60 MU. 18.9.67 Wattisham for onward delivery by 111 Sqn to 56 Sqn, becoming 'P' 56 Sqn by 30.10.67. 20.10.71 60 MU. 22.8.72 'M' 111 Sqn. 24.6.74 crashed North Sea off Gt Yarmouth after hydraulics failure.

XR749 c/n 95214. f/f 30.4.65. Retained BAC and partially modified by F6, then de-modded to F3. 4.10.67 60 MU. By 30.10.67 'Q' 56 Sqn. 26.10.71 60 MU. 30.10.72 Binbrook. 21.11.72 'Q' 5 Sqn. 6.76 store. 2.77 'Q' 5 Sqn. 5.78 store. 10.78 'Q' 5 Sqn. 30.1.80 store. 2.8.82 St Athan, returning 16.8.82 in light grey scheme, then LAF, and store. By 14.12.82 'BM' 11 Sqn. 3.83 store. 5.83 'BM' 11 Sqn. 11.84 'BO' 11 Sqn. 1.85 'DC' LTF. 2.85 'DA' LTF. 1.10.85 Blue fin and spine in 10th anniversary of LTF scheme. 3.86 store. 19.5.86 marked in 'Q' 56 Sqn commemorative scheme. By 14.11.86 markings removed, but still coded 'Q' with 'D' type roundels used by all three Binbrook units sporadically until 17.2.87 when took off en route for Lossiemouth, only to make emergency landing at Leuchars where allocated 8934M for battle damage repair duties.

XR750 c/n 95215. f/f 10.5.65. Retained BAC. 9.10.67 60 MU. 3.1.69 'A' 56 Sqn. 22.9.71 '750' 226 OCU. Early 9.74 'N' 111 Sqn. 10.74 Wattisham store. 1.75 SOC and scrapped.

XR751 c/n 95216. f/f 31.5.65. Retained BAC. 19.1.68 60 MU. 2.71 '751' 226 OCU. 1.4.71 'Q' 29 Sqn. 10.72 'N' 5 Sqn, then 'R' 5 Sqn. 1.79 LTF after store. 23.3.79 'C' LTF. 23.9.79 'A' LTF. 3.9.82 St Athan, returning 22.9.82 in light grey scheme, then stored, until late 87. By 4.88 scrapped. (2,060hr.)

LIGHTNING T4

XL628 c/n 95049. f/f 6.5.59 (prototype P11). Reatined trials EE. 1.10.59 crashed over Irish Sea when fin broke off after high-speed roll. Test pilot J. Squier ejected successfully while aircraft supersonic. (40.51min.)

XL629 c/n 95050. f/f 29.9.59 (second prototype P11). Retained by EE. 13.5.66 ETPS coded '23'. Withdrawn from use 1.76, displayed on gate Boscombe Down.

XM966 c/n 95051. f/f 15.7.60 Samlesbury-Filton where converted to T5. f/f as T5 1.12.62. Retained EE. 22.7.65 crashed on test over Irish Sea after fin disintegrated following structural failure at Mach 2.0. Test pilots ejected safely. (152.51hr.)

XM967 c/n 95052. Built T4 but not flown as such. Moved by road to Filton for conversion to first T5, f/f 30.3.62. Used EE/BAC, A&AEE and RAE Farnborough trials until 6.74, sent Honington fire compound. Reprieved, flown RAF Colerne 5.1.75 for preservation, but scrapped 5 MU Kemble 7.76.

XM968 c/n 95053. f/f 9.11.60. Retained EE/BAC until 9.64. 2.8.65 6O MU. 4.66 968/226 OCU. Mid-71 60 MU. 2.72 'Q' 92 Sqn. Allocated 8541M, but crashed near Gütersloh 24.2.77.

XM969 c/n 95054. f/f 28.3.61. 29.6.62 'H' LCS. 1.6.63 '969' 226 OCU. 20.7.74 Binbrook store. 16.4.75 dumped as decoy, 8592M, burnt 1982.

XM970 c/n 95055. f/f 5.5.61. 27.6.62 'G' LCS. 1.6.63 '970' 226 OCU. Loaned 19/92 Sqns 63/64. 7.74 60 MU hack. 23.7.76 'T' 19 Sqn. 31.12.76 allocated 8529M, transferred RAF Brüggen as decoy, later scrapped.

XM971 c/n 95071. f/f 23.6.61. 23.7.62 'K' LCS. 1.6.63 '971' 226 OCU. 2.1.67 crashed Tunstead, near Coltishall, after radome collapsed and debris entered air intake. (688.30hr.)

XM972 c/n 95072. f/f 29.4.61. 2.7.62 'J' LCS. 1.6.63 '972' 226 OCU. Lent to 19/92 Sqns 9.72-4.73 before returning 226 OCU. 11.6.74 Waddington for fire practice. Dumped 81.

XM973 c/n 95073. f/f 17.5.61. 3.8.62 'K' AFDS. Spring 63 lent to 74 Sqn and 111 Sqn. 2.64 'T' 111 Sqn. 10.64 'T' 23 Sqn, re-coded 'Z' 23 Sqn by 2.65. 2.66 '973' 226 OCU. 13.10.72 60 MU. 29.9.72 'V' 19 Sqn until 31.12.76 when transferred RAF Brüggen as decoy as 8528M, later scrapped.

XM974 c/n 95074. f/f 19.6.61. 8.62 'J' AFDS. Lent 74 Sqn as 'T' early 63, transfer to 'T' 74 Sqn by 9.63. 3.66 '974' 226 OCU. 14.12.72 crashed North Sea, 35 miles off Happisburgh, Norfolk, after reheat fire. (1,753hr.)

XM987 c/n 95075. f/f 13.7.61. 29.8.62 LCS (uncoded). 1.6.63 '987' 226 OCU. 24.6.74 Conningsby. Retained for Lincs Air Museum, Tattershall, but not transferred; used battle damage repair training, then scrapped.

XM988 c/n 95076. f/f 21.8.61. 29.10.62 'O' 19 Sqn. 12.62 'T' 19 Sqn. 8.63 '988' 226 OCU. 9.63 lent to 74 Sqn until early 64. 5.6.73 crashed North Sea.

XM989 c/n 95077. f/f 30.8.61. 5.9.62 'Z' 56 Sqn, recoded 'X' 56 Sqn by 15.9.62. 3.64 60 MU. 6.4.66 Warton after repurchase by BAC for conversion to T54. 6.6.66 delivered Saudi Arabia via Wattisham as '54-650', later re-serialled '54-607' and preserved at Dhahran.

XM990 c/n 95078. f/f 21.9.61. 20.9.62 LCS (uncoded, then '990'). 1.6.63 '990' 226 OCU. 19.9.70 suffered control failure during Battle of Britain air show, Coltishall, crashed South Walsham, Norfolk. (1,282hr.)

XM991 c/n 95079. f/f 4.10.61. 13.10.62 LCS (uncoded, then '991'). 1.6.63 '991' 226 OCU. 8.63 'T' 19 Sqn. Allocated 8456M, burnt out in ground fire at Gütersloh 6.75.

XM992 c/n 95080. f/f 13.12.61. 24.9.62 'Z' 111 Sqn. 7.4.66 delivered Warton after purchase by BAC for conversion to T54. 6.6.66 delivered Saudiu Arabia via Wattisham as '54-651', later re-serialled '54-608'. Dumped Khamis Mushayt.

XM993 c/n 95100. f/f 9.12.61. 13.10.62 LCS (never coded). 12.12.62 overran runway and overturned, Middleton-St-George, returning from Chivenor. 14.12.62 SOC, parts St Athan.

XM994 c/n 95101. f/f 12.3.62. 6.11.62 19 Sqn (to aid conversion to Lightnings of 19/92 Sqns). 7.3.63 LCS. 8.5.63-27.6.63 lent to Leconfield (19/92 Sqns). 27.6.63 994/226 OCU. 6.74 60 MU disposal. 29.4.75 West Raynham dump. Scrapped 77.

XM995 c/n 95104. f/f 25.1.62. 29.11.62 'T' 19 Sqn. 25.3.69 60 MU. 3.12.69 'T' 92 Sqn. 6.4.77 Wildenrath as decoy, allocated 8542M.

XM996 c/n 95103 f/f 13.4.62. 29.1.63 LCS (uncoded, then '996'). 1.6.63 '996' 226 OCU. 6.74 withdrawn from use, flown to Manston for fire practice, scrapped.

XM997 c/n 95111. f/f 22.5.62. 22.2.63 LCS (uncoded, then '997'). 1.6.63 '997' 226 OCU. 8.7.74 60 MU. Used for rescue practice Leconfield until 11.76 when transferred Catterick Fire School for burning.

LIGHTNING T5

XS416 c/n B1/95001. f/f 20.8.64. Retained by BAC and A&AEE. 26.7.65 '416' 226 OCU. By 11.65 to 74 Sqn, becoming 'T'. 1.67 'T' 11 Sqn. 8.72 first T5 to exceed 1,000 flying hours. 19.4.74 60 MU. 12.74 'Z' 11 Sqn. 28.10.74 'T' 11 Sqn. 5.77 store. 26.4.78 'V' LTF. 2.81 'DU' LTF. 6.83 store. 31.10.83 St Athan, returning 11.11.83 in light grey scheme, stored. 4.84 'AT' 5 Sqn. 19.7.84 starboard u/c collapsed on landing, causing all T5s to fly with u/c down for some weeks until problem solved. 2.7.85 after repair 'AZ' 5 Sqn. Active until 12.87. In store 29.3.88. Scrapped 4.88. (3,088hr.)

XS417 c/n B1/95002. f/f 17.7.64. Retained BAC and A&AEE. 25.5.65 '417' 226 OCU. 2.66 'Z' 23 Sqn (lent 226 OCU 10.70-4.71). 9.75 60 MU then 'Z' 56 Sqn. 7.76 60 MU. 8.76 LTF, becoming 'W'. 1.80 'T' 11 Sqn. 10.80 'BT' 11 Sqn. 5.82 store. 2.83 'DZ' LTF. 13.3.84 damaged when ventral tank struck runway, on take-off. 6.84 repaired and resprayed, 'DZ' LTF. 4.87 withdrawn from use, stored until 12.87. Scrapped 3.88. (2,630hr.)

XS418 c/n B1/95003. f/f 12.11.64. 30.3.65 A&AEE. 7.8.65 '418' 226 OCU. 23.8.68 u/c retracted on landing at Stradishall. 9.1.69 returned Coltishall, 226 OCU. 22.8.74 Binbrook store. 3.11.75 decoy (allocated 8531M). 10.77 camouflaged. Scrapped late 87.

XS419 c/n B1/95004. f/f 18.12.64. 29.3.65 A&AEE. 20.4.65 '419' 226 OCU. 23.7.74 'T' 23 Sqn. 3.11.75 Binbrook store. 9.76 'X' LTF. 24.1.78 'T' 5 Sqn. 2.79 store. 5.80 'W', then 'DW' LTF. 2.81 'DW' 23 Sqn, returning 9.12.82 in light grey scheme. 5.83 'DV' LTF. 2.87 withdrawn from use, stored until late 87. Scrapped early 88. (2,608hr.)

XS420 c/n B1/95005. f/f 23.1.65. 29.4.65 '420' 226 Sqn OCU. 23.9.74 Binbrook store. 18.9.76 'T' (at Coningsby), 'V' LTF by 1.77. 20.3.78 landing accident, Binbrook, Cat 3. 7.3.79 repaired, to IRRU 7.79 'Y' LTF. 5.80 store. 1.81 'DV' LTF. Stored until erly 88. Scrapped by 4.88.

XS421 c/n B1/95006. f/f 25.2.65. 11.5.65 '421' 226 OCU. 4.5.71 'T' 111 Sqn. 23.11.71 60 MU. 9.72 'T' 111 Sqn. 11.74 'S' 23 Sqn. 23.4.75 60 MU. 5.75 'S' 23 Sqn. 22.10.75 Binbrook, open store, then decoy. 24.9.76 wingless airframe to Boscombe Down by road for FOD injection tests (allocated 8503M). 27.9.76 P&EE/AWRE Foulness.

XS422 c/n B1/95007. f/f 24.3.65. 1.6.65 '422' 226 OCU. 3.69 conducted first air-to-air T5 refuellings by OCU. 9.69 'O' 29 Sqn. 1.70 60 MU. 8.70 'T' 111 Sqn, considered something of a 'rogue' aircraft. 20.5.71 60 MU. 15.3.72 'Z' 29 Sqn. 12.72 'Z' 56 Sqn. 1.76 ETPS, Boscombe Down, acquiring red fin, spine and wing decor 8.76. Reported out of hours late 87. Withdrawn by 4.88.

XS423 c/n B1/95008. f/f 31.5.65. 1.6.65 '423' 226 OCU. Lent to 23 Sqn 19.4.66-3.3.67. 16.3.67 BAC Warton. 9.67 226 OCU. 2.73 A&AEE trials. 2.9.74 Binbrook store. 11.75 open store, then decoy, camouflaged 10.77, alloted 8532M. Scrapped late 87.

XS449 c/n B1/95009. f/f 30.4.65. 17.7.65 '449' 226 OCU. 7.66 (approx)-9.11.66 lent 74 Sqn. 3.69 damaged flying through thunderstorm. 2.9.74 Binbrook store. 11.75 decoy (allocated 8533M). Scrap status 87.

XS450 c/n B1/95010. f/f 25.5.65. 6.9.65 'T' 111 Sqn. 7.70 60 MU. 9.70 '450' 226 OCU. 2.9.74 Binbrook store. 1.1.75 5 Sqn (unmarked). 3.11.75 open store 8.11.75 decoy, camouflaged 10.77, allocated 8534M scrapped late 87.

XS451 c/n B1/95011. f/f 3.6.65. 7.65 AFDS (uncoded). 18.11.65 'T' 5 Sqn (dayglo 'T' bands) 6.71 60 MU. 24.11.71 '451' 226 OCU. 22.8.74 'X' 11 Sqn ('C' Flt). 5.11.75 LTF. 25.11.76 St Atha ground instructional airframe, allocated 8503M 6.78 RAF Newton missile instruction. 88 removec for restoration.

XS452 c/n B1/95012. f/f 30.6.65. 20.9.65 '452' 22€ OCU. 3.2.71 60 MU. 11.11.71 'T' 111 Sqn. 12.7 re-coded 'X' 111 Sqn. 2.74 'X' 56 Sqn. 1.75 Akrotir Station Flight (Flamingo on pink fin, pink-blue nos markings), used APC-detached UK Lightnin squadrons. 21.5.75 Binbrook, store. 7.75 'Y' 11 Sq ('C' Flt). First flight in dark green experimenta camouflage 18.7.75. 11.75 LTF. 5.4.76 lent 5 Sqn 10.76 store. 7.77 'T' 11 Sqn. 7.80 'Z' LTF. 11.80 'DZ LTF. 15.2.83 St Athan returning 2.3.83 in light grey scheme, and stored. 1.4.85 'BT' 11 Sqn. 30.6.8 Cranfield, purchased by Mr Arnold Glass.

XS453 c/n B1/95013. f/f 6.7.65. 10.9.65 '453' 226 OCU. 1.6.66 crashed North Sea off Happisburgh Norfolk after hydraulic failure. (30.30hr.)

XS454 c/n B1/95014. f/f 6.7.65. 9.10.65 'T' 74 Sqn 12.65 '454' 226 OCU. 7.3.67 Cat 3 after u/c retractec on landing, Coltishall (208hr). 2.68 repaired. 8.73 lent to 5/11 Sqns at Leconfield. 15.8.74 'Y' 11 Sqn 7.75 store. 11.75 decoy, allocated 8535M. 8.84 fire dump. Scrapped 87.

XS455 c/n B1/95015. f/f 23.9.65. 20.12.65 '455' 226 OCU. 25.3.68 u/c collapsed on landing at Wattisham. 9.10.69 60 MU. 2.70 '455' 226 OCU. 27.7.71 'T' 5 Sqn. 6.9.72 crashed North Sea off Withensea following hydraulics failure (1,085.50hr.)

XS456 c/n B1/95016. f/f 26.10.65. 20.12.65 'A 56 Sqn. 8.69 'X' 56 Sqn. 23.2.73 60 MU. 16.4.74 'T 11 Sqn, later 'Z' 11 Sqn ('C' Flt). 10.76 open store 2.77 LTF, coded 'T' by 5.77. 11.80 'DT' LTF. 8.85 store. 2.86 'DX' LTF. Stored 5.87. Scrapped early 88. (2,314hr.)

XS457 c/n B1/95017. f/f 8.11.65. 21.12.66 '457' 226 OCU. 8.69 lent 23 Sqn. 24.11.71 60 MU. 14.8.72 '457' 226 OCU. 15.8.74 'W' 11 Sqn ('C' Flt). 10.75 LTF. 8.78 'Y' LTF. 7.79 store. 18.7.79 A&AEE/ETPS 27.2.81 Binbrook store. 6.8.81 'AT' 5 Sqn. 9.12.83 damaged after aircraft left runway when starboard u/c collapsed in wet weather landing. Stored until late 87. Scrapped 4.88.

XS458 c/n B1/95018. f/f 3.12.65. 2.2.66 '458' 226 OCU. 4.72 5 Sqn. 8.73 OCU. 2.9.74 Binbrook store. 9.75 dark grey experimental camouflage, issued to LTF, becoming 'Z' LTF by 9.76. 12.1.79 'T' 5 Sqn. 10.80 'AT' 5 Sqn. 5.82 'BT' 11 Sqn. 5.3.85 'DX' LTF. 8.86 store. 10.86 'DY' LTF. 5.87 5 Sqn (as 'DY' LTF) until 12.87, when transferred 11 Sqn, still marked as 'DY' LTF. 30.6.88 Cranfield, purchased by Mr Arnold Glass.

XS459 c/n B1/95019. f/f 18.12.65. 13.3.66 '459' 226 OCU. 19.5.71 60 MU. 29.2.72 'T' 29 Sqn. 2.75 'X' 56 Sqn. 5.76 LTF (as 'X' 56 Sqn). 10.76 store. 4.78 'X' LTF. 1.80 'DX' LTF. 27.3.81 badly damaged Binbrook in landing accident, repaired but did not fly again until 13.3.84. 'DW' LTF, in use as such, with 5 and 11 Sqns 2.87. Store 12.87. Scrapped by 4.88. (2,306hr.)

XS460 c/n B1/95020. f/f 2.2.66. Converted to T55, serialled '55-710'. Written off 7.3.67 Warton, in cross-wind landing accident. (14.53hr.)

XV328 c/n B1/95021. f/f 22.12.66. 31.1.67 60 MU. 3.67 'Z' 29 Sqn. 10.69 badly damaged Coltishall while on detachment. 2.70 'Z' 29 Sqn. 8.3.72 60 MU. 19.1.73 'T' 5 Sqn. 3.80 'Y' LTF. 11.80 'DY' LTF. 9.12.82 St Athan, returning 6.1.83 in light grey scheme, stored. 10.83 'DU' LTF. 4.87 'BZ' 11 Sqn. 30.6.88 Cranfield, purchased by Mr Arnold Glass.

XV329 c/n B1/95022. f/f 30.12.66. 28.2.67 60 MU. 3.3.67 Shorts, Sydenham for preparation for despatch to Singapore. 8.3.67 shipped to 390 MU, Singapore, aboard MV *Calchas*, suffering some salt corrosion en route, arriving 10.4.67. 1.7.67 'T' 74 Sqn. 10.71 Sydenham aboard MV *Robert Middleton*. 14.12.71 flown 60 MU, Leconfield. 21.12.71 noted Coltishall. 3.74 SOC due acid spillage from batteries and excessive salt corrosion to tailplane, scrapped Leconfield 5.74, still 'T' 74 Sqn.

LIGHTNING F6

XP693 c/n 95116. f/f 16.6.62 as F3.1.67. converted '3A (Interim F6) at Warton 1.11.67 A&AEE height and heading lock programme on flight 263 (212hr 3min). 19.1.69 BAC Warton. 2.69 A&AEE F6 development. 1972 MRCA (Tornado) trials Warton, then A&AEE intermittently. Early 76 RAF Valley missile trials, Aberporth Range. 28.1.77, chase plane at Warton for Tornado IDS 30.1.81 resumed flying after storage, as chase for Tornado F2 development. 21.8.85 seen with white paint on port underside and rear aft of wing root — later removed. Operated from Warton on Tornado F3 development 86/87. Currently active.

XP697 c/n 95151. f/f 18.7.63. 13.8.63 flown Filton on second flight for conv to F3A (Interim F6). 17.4.64 f/f as F6, Filton-Warton for development. 2.11.64 Handling, auto pilot, telemetry trials. 5.66 A&AEE 2in rocket tests 8.67 Avon 302C performance trials. 7.68 A&AEE, 12.68 Warton. 23.2.70 MinTech charge. 14.4.70 60 MU overhaul. 13.5.70 Warton. 1971/2 speed profile tests with over-wing tanks, and refuelling probe. 7.72 MRCA development work. 15.12.75 Binbrook for store, acquired camouflage and 11 Sqn marks by 9.77. 3.10.78 Warton, used fatigue test rig to evaluate extending F6 service life (Lightning Support Flying programme). 6.5.83 completed. 9.83 scrapped.

XR723 c/n 95206. f/f 2.2.65, as F3, Salmesbury-Warton. Stored, conv to F6 9.6.67 to 'L' 11 Sqn. 29.11.67 endurance flight 8hr 15min with five AARs, pilot Flt Lt W. D. E. Eggleton. 22.3.72 60 MU overhaul and store. 6.73 to 'K' 23 Sqn. 9.73 re-coded 'F' 23 Sqn 7.74 re-coded 'A' 23 Sqn 9.8.74 60 MU overhaul. late 74 to 'F' 23 sqn. 3.11.75 Binbrook. 3.76 'D' 5 Sqn; in and out of store, camouflaged. 9.78 'A' 5 Sqn. 18.9.79 crashed into sea 15 miles south of RAF Akrotiri after engine fire. Pilot (Gp Capt P. Carter) ejected safely, returned to dry land within ½hr.

XR724 c/n 95207. f/f 10.2.65 as F3, Salmesbury-Warton. Stored, conv to F6. 16.6.67 to 'M' 11 Sqn. 4.3.72 60 MU overhaul 5.72 'M' 11 Sqn 11.8.72 re-coded 'K' 11 Sqn. 3.76 Cat 3 damage when starter exploded, Binbrook. 17.7.76 Leconfield 'temp base for 11 Sqn) as 'K' 11 Sqn 1.6.79 Binbrook display a/c, 5 Sqn marks one side, 11 Sqn the other. 12.79 'K' LTF. 13.1.81 'AG' 5 Sqn. 14.7.82 re-code AV', later reverted to 'AG'. 19.10.82 St Athan light grey respray. 9.11.82 returned from St Athan with transposed serial XR742(!) as 'AG' 5. 11.83 'BC' 11 Sqn. Intermittent storage until 2.4.86. 17.4.86 'AE' 5 Sqn. 3.6.86 St Athan dark grey respray, returning 19.6.86, rejoining as 'AE' 5 Sqn. 5.87 stored Binbrook. 8.87 'AE' 5 Sqn remained in use until disbandment 12.87, then fitted with over-wing tanks and used for BAe Tornado F3 radar trials (still as 'AE' 29.3.88). 11.4.88 to BAe Warton for continuation of trials. Current.

XR725 c/n 95208. f/f 19.2.65 as F3, Salmesbury-Warton. Stored, conv to F6. 15.8.67 60 MU. 16.8.67 Warton, then 'A' 23 Sqn same day. 26.10.67 taxying accident (port u/c sank through concrete) while detached to Sola, Norway, flown 60 MU for repair, then 'A' 28.8.68 Toronto 7hr 20min for air show returning 3.9.68. 1.70 store (60 MU?). 7.70 'A' 74 Sqn. 14.9.71 60 MU, overhaul. 25.4.72 'Y' 56 Sqn delivered via 23 Sqn. 4.75 re-coded 'P' 56 Sqn 13.1.76 60 MU overhaul. 25.5.76 'J' 5 Sqn. 7.78 stored. 6.5.80 'F' LTF, 11.80 re-coded 'DF' LTF. 3.81 stored. 5.82 St Athan light grey re-spray, returning 27.5.82 as 'DF' LTF. 8.82 store. 9.82 LAF. 15.10.85 'BA' 11 Sqn. 11.5.87 black fin, soon extended to spine. 12.87 store. Scrapped 4.88. (3,870.20hr.)

XR726 c/n 95209. f/f 26.2.65 as F3 Salmesbury-Warton. Stored and conv to F6 12.7.67 60 MU, used by Stn Flt. 14.11.67 first noted with 'Golden Arrow' markings. 1.2.68 loaned 23 Sqn (unmarked). 29.2.68 'N' 5 Sqn. 24.10.72 60 MU overhaul. 10.1.73 'N' 5 Sqn. 19.10.73 damaged by No2 engine starter fire Binbrook (1,693hr 15min). 7.8.76 stored. 23.2.68 'K' 5 Sqn. 3.8.79 painted 'K' 23 Sqn for 25th anniversary. 15.8.79 lost rudder in flight, landed safely. 7.80 stored. 12.80 'AE' 5 Sqn. 5.81 stored. 8.12.81 St Athan respray, returned 11.2.82 light grey scheme, stored/used LAF with whom coded 'F' in red dayglo. 3.83 'DF' LTF. 12.83 stored. 15.4.85 air tested following 30-week mod programme Binbrook by BAe to extend fatigue life by 400hr. 'BE' 11 Sqn same month. 6.86 stored then 'DF' LTF

until 26.3.87. 30.4.87 'BM' 11 Sqn. 7.87. Withdrawn from use, stripped for spares. (3,976.25hr.)

XR727 c/n 95210. f/f 8.3.65 as F3 Salmesbury-Warton. Stored, conv F6. 15.9.67 'L' 23 Sqn, re-coded 'F' 23 sqn by 11.67. 10.8.73 60 MU overhaul 4.12.73 air tested, brakes failed on landing and ran off Leconfield runway sustaining Cat 3 damage (1,480hr 5min). 13.12.73 'F' 11 Sqn. 11.78 stored. 9.80 'G' 11 Sqn, re-coded 'BG' 11 Sqn by 12.80. 6.81 stored. 12.6.82 St Athan light grey respray returning 2.8.82 when used LAF. 10.3.84 'AB' 5 Sqn. 15.1.86 loaned 11 Sqn. 22.1.86 stored 25.9.86 'AB' 5 Sqn. 9.87 'BH' 11 Sqn. 5.88 Wildenrath BDR.

XR728 c/n 95211. f/f 17.3.65 as F3, Salmesbury-Warton for store, conv to F6. 1.11.67 'D' 23 Sqn. 13.5.71 60 MU overhaul 24.11.71 'D' 56 Sqn, delivered Akrotiri via 5 Sqn. 2.7.75 60 MU overhaul. 24.10.75 'J' 56 Sqn. 1.7.76 Binbrook store. 12.7.78 air tested, white code 'J'. 7.78 'D' LTF, later re-coded 'DD' LTF. 4.81 stored. 6.81 'AF' 5 Sqn 12.11.81 St Athan respray (camouflage). By 2.82 'BA' 11 Sqn. 2.8.83 St Athan dark grey respray, returning 28.8.83, placed store with short spells with 5 and 11 Sqns. 6.85 'BF' 11 Sqn. 16.6.87 'BS' 11 Sqn. By 9.7.87 re-coded 'JS' as mount for Binbrook Station Commander, Gp Capt John Spencer, with LTF-style fin markings. 24.6.88 Last flight, flown to Bruntingthorpe for Lightning Preservation Group.

XR747 c/n 95212. f/f 2.4.65 as F3, Salmesbury-Warton for store and conv to F6. Late 67 to 60 MU storage. 4.1.68 'K' 23 Sqn. 4.6.73 60 MU overhaul. 20.9.73 'K' 23 Sqn. 15.5.74 'X' 111 Sqn. 30.9.74 Binbrook. 11.74 'P' Sqn. 2.76 first 5 Sqn to receive grey/green camouflage scheme. 16.2.77 re-coded 'E' 5 Sqn. 9.77 Cat 3 with persistent fuel leaks, placed in store until 10/78 when returned to service as 'E' 5 sqn. 4.79 stored. 5.6.81 due to be placed on fire dump, Binbrook but fell off low-loader and left on belly ('5' Sqn marks), and used as 'photo mount' for 'Families Day' 6.6.81. Repaired, 18.5.82 air tested and transferred to LAF as 'X' 8.82 'BF' 11 Sqn. 2.85, Mod, 9 to give 400 more flying hours. 23.8.85 air tested. 24.9.85 'AL' 5 Sqn. 7.8.87 Lost part of rudder in flight, made emergency landing, Coningsby. 22.8.87 (last flight) to Binbrook. Scrapped 4.88. (3,650.40hr.)

XR752 c/n 95217. f/f 16.6.65 as F3A, Salmesbury-Warton for store. 26.11.65 'V' AFDS. 6.67 'U' 23 Sqn, later re-coded 'C' 23 Sqn. 20.10.67 BAC, Warton conv full F6. 24.10.68 Leuchars pool coded 'W'. 1.7.70 'G' 23 Sqn. 7.73 60 MU overhaul. 17.8.73 'G' 23 Sqn. 15.5.74 'Y' 111 Sqn. 15.10.74 'B' 5 Sqn 16.12.75 store. 3.76 'H' 5 Sqn. 22.4.76 60 MU overhaul. 11.76 Binbrook store. 9.77 'H' 5 Sqn. 29.9.77 Cat 2 wheels up landing Binbrook (first F6 to do so), cost £99,000 to repair. 25.1.78 air tested. 6.78 'D' 11 Sqn. 9.80 'E' 5 Sqn then 'BH' 11 Sqn by 11.80. 3.82 store. 1.4.82 St Athan light grey respray,

returning 21.4.82, stored. Temporarily used 5 Sqn without codes, periodically 83 and 84. 5.84 'BL' 11 Sqn. 11.85 stored after suffering fire on landing. 22.4.87 decoy, scrapped by 9.87.

XR753 c/n 95218. f/f 23.6.65 as F3A, Salmesbury-Warton for store. 16.11.65 33 MU store. 26.11.65. 'T' AFDS. 2.66 re-coded 'U' FCTU 10.8.67 23 Sqn becoming 'V' 23 Sqn. 21.3.68 BAC Warton mod to full F6. 18.7.69 60 MU. 9.69 'B' 5 Sqn. 3.71 60 MU overhaul. 16.8.71 Leuchars. 21.8.71 'A' 23 Sqn mid-74 60 MU overhaul. 9.8.74 'A' 23 sqn. 3.11.75 Coningsby. 12.11.75 'F' 5 Sqn (Binbrook). 15.6.76 60 MU overhaul early 10.76 'A' 5 Sqn, during 1980 used by LTF. 6.81 'BA' 11 Sqn. 4.83 'AG' 5 Sqn. 11.84 store. 28.3.85 'AC' 5 Sqn. 2.86 uncoded 5 Sqn, by 10.86 'BP' 11 sqn. 24.5.88 Leeming for BDR (3,487.20hr).

XR754 c/n 25219. f/f 8.7.65 as F3A Salmesbury-Warton for storage. 3.12.65 Handling Sqn/A&AEE. 2.2.66 'G' 5 Sqn. 31.1.67 BAC Warton mod to full F6 (296hr 7min). 29.2.68 'M' 23 Sqn. 13.11.70 60 MU overhaul. 5.71 'M' 23 Sqn 7.71 re-coded 'D' 23 Sqn. 3.11.75 Binbrook. 21.4.76 'E' 11 Sqn. 17.7.76 'D' 5 Sqn. By 7.77 'A' 11 Sqn. By 4.81 'AE' 5 Sqn. 6.1.83 St Athan light grey respray, returning 25.1.83, placed in store. 20.8.84 'AE' 5 Sqn. (21.8.84 departed APC Akrotiri, when 'sharksteeth' markings applied). 3.86 stored. 10.12.86 'BC' 11 Sqn. 'BC' 11 Sqn by 8.87. 24.6.88 Wattisham for BDR.

XR755 c/n 95220. f/f 15.7.65 as F3A Salmesbury-Warton for storage. 10.12.65 33 MU store, issued soon afterwards as 'G' 5 Sqn. 3.66 re-coded 'A' 5 Sqn. 7.4.67 BAC, Warton mod, to full F6. (321hr 35min). 3.5.68 f/f as F6. 25.5.68 'O' 5 Sqn. mid-71 60 MU overhaul. 11.7.72 returned 5 Sqn, later coded 'O'. 8.73 BAC Warton. 1.74 'A' 5 Sqn. 17.7.75 re-coded 'D' 5 Sqn. 13.2.76 60 MU overhaul. 15.6.76 5 sqn, coded 'F' 5 Sqn by 11.76. By 9.78 stored. By 1.80 'J' Sqn. By 11.80 'BJ' 11 Sqn. 11.81 store. 12.83 'BF' 11 Sqn. (f/f as such 2.2.84). 3.84 store 5.84 'BF' 11 Sqn by 6.85 store. 3.86 'BN' 11 Sqn. 1.87 store. By 8.87 'BN'/11 Sqn. Last flown 12.87. Salvaged 4.88 (4,093.30hr). 24.6.88 Castle Air, Cornwall.

XR756 c/n 95221. f/f 11.8.65 as F3A, Salmesbury-Warton, for storage. 10.12.65 'B' 5 Sqn. 19.4.67 BAC Warton mod to F6. 13.6.68 Leuchars 401hr 9min). 14.9.68 Leuchars pool as 'U', flying with 11 Sqn. 23.2.70 60 MU overhaul and storage 14.12.70 'H' 23 Sqn. 1.71 re-coded 'M' 23 Sqn, 20.8.73 damaged when venting fuel from No 1 engine caused flash fire on ground (1,722hr 5min). 20.9.74 60 MU overhaul. 6.2.75 'M' 23 Sqn. 3.11.75 Binbrook, store. 3.76 used by both 5 and 11 Sqns. 21.4.76 60 MU and became 'M' of Leconfield Pool. 21.6.76 11 Sqn (Coningsby) coded 'J' by 8.76. 28.1.77 store. 5.79 'G' Sqn. By 10.79 re-coded 'AG' 5 Sqn. 1.81 store. LAF (coded 'F') by 29.7.82. 11.1.83 LTF. 2.83 'BB' 11 Sqn. 3.85 store. 26.9.85 'BH' 11 Sqn. Last flown 6.87. Salvaged 4.88 (3,889.50hr).

Below:

XR752 'H' of 5 Squadron, 'grounded' at Binbrook after a unique wheels-up landing on 29 September 1977 by the CO, which was quite a feat of airmanship! The F6 travelled almost 6,000ft down the runway on its belly tank with minimal damage. The starboard Red Top has been removed as it was a live missile, whereas the port weapon was only an acquisition round. Category 2 damage was repaired at a cost of £99,000 and '752 was back in the air on 25 January 1978. *Via Dave Tuplin*

XR757 c/n 95222. f/f 19.8.65 as F3A, Salmesbury-Warton, for store. Late 5.67 'R' 23 sqn. 26.1.68 BAC Warton for mod to F6. 21.2.69. 60 MU store. By 9.69 Leuchars Pool as 'V' 2.70 'D' 11 Sqn then 60 MU overhaul same month. 4.5.71 'D' 11 Sqn. 13.1.75 60 MU overhaul. 6.6.75 'D' 11 Sqn. 17.7.76 store. 11.78 'A' 11 Sqn. 7.80 store. 4.81 5 Sqn (uncoded). 4.1.82 St Athan light grey respray with white underwing serials!), returning 26.1.82, into store. By 6.82 'Y' LAF. 8.82 'BE' 11 Sqn. 9.83 St Athan dark grey respray returning 10.10.83, placed into store. 24.2.84 5 Sqn (uncoded), 29.6.84 11 Sqn marks, 7.84 'AL' 5 Sqn. 24.9.85 'BA' 11 Sqn. 10.85 store. 2.7.86 5 Sqn marks applied. 7.86 'BL' 11 Sqn. Last flown 12.87. Salvaged 4.88 (4,316hr).

XR758 c/n 95223. f/f 30.8.65 as F3A Salmesbury-Warton, for store. 11.1.66 'D' 5 Sqn. 10.66 'U' 23 Sqn. 16.3.67 BAC Warton mod to F6. 24.4.68 11 Sqn, but allocated to Leuchars Pool (Command Reserve) coded 'V'. 1.69 'J' 74 Sqn. 11.69 Cat 4 starter explosion Darwin, Australia. 16.1.70 air-lifted RAF Belfast transport aircraft BAC Warton for repair. 26.4.71 'E' 23 Sqn. 26.9.73 60 MU overhaul. 18.12.73 Binbrook, and 'B' 5 Sqn next day. 9.10.74 Cat 3R after low landing at Binbrook which scraped off after-burner unit. 7.1.77 f/f since 11.74. 28.1.77 'J' 11 Sqn. 8.78 store. 4.79 'E' 5 Sqn. 8.80 re-coded 'AE' 5 Sqn then 'F' 5 Sqn. 12.80 store. 27.4.81 'AF' 5 Sqn, 6.81 store. 6.12.83 'M' 5 Sqn. 1.84. 'AH' 5 Sqn. 8.85 store. 6.86 'BF' 11 Sqn. 26.3.87 'DF' LTF, returned store few days later. 5.87 'BF' 11 Sqn. 9.87 Current. 12.5.88 Laarbruch BDR, as 8964 M.

XR759 c/n 95224. f/f 9.9.65 as F3A, Salmesbury-Warton for storage. 18.1.66 'E' 5 Sqn. 27.2.67 replaced and to 60 MU overhaul. 18.7.67 BAC Warton for mod to full F6. (274hr 45min.) 2.8.68 60 MU store. 1.11.68 'R' 5 Sqn. 6.70 'A' 5 Sqn. 6.71 'G' 74 Sqn at Leuchars. 30.8.71 'P' 56 Sqn. 9.6.72 60 MU overhaul. 26.10.72 'P' 56 Sqn. 26.6.75 Binbrook store. 14.7.75 'P' 11 Sqn. 8.12.75 re-coded 'H' 11 Sqn. 9.77 store. 8.8.78 'H' 5 Sqn. 3.10. 79 lent to 11 Sqn for APC, Akrotiri with dayglo red code 'B'. 8.11.79 returned to 'H' 5 Sqn, later 'AH' 5 Sqn, then stored late 81. 11.2.82 St Athan light grey respray, returning 3.3.82. 14.5.82 LAF. 6.82 used as 11 Sqn display aircraft. 8.82 returned to 'AH' 5 Sqn. 31.1.84 St Athan respray in dark grey scheme, returning 29.2.84 into store. 15.5.85 'BJ' 11 Sqn. Active 24.9.87, withdrawn end 8.87 for spares. Scrapped 4.88. (3,748.35hr.)

XR760 c/n 95225. f/f 20.9.65 as F3A, Salmesbury-Warton for storage. 27.1.66 'F' 5 Sqn. 9.1.67 BAC Warton mod to F6. (297hr 40min.) 9.10.67 60 MU store. 28.11.67 'H' 23 Sqn. 25.9.70 60 MU overhaul. 3.3.71 'H' 23 Sqn. 9.10.73 undershot and hit

approach lights, Luqa, Malta (1,846hr 55min). 3.11.75 Binbrook store. 8.3.76 60 MU overhaul. 7.76 5 Sqn coded 'G' 5 Sqn by 8.76. 7.77 re-coded 'B' 5 Sqn. 6.78 store. 4.81 5 Sqn (uncoded). 27.4.81 St Athan respray (in light grey scheme.) by 7.81, with 5 Sqn (uncoded). 3.82 'AA' 5 Sqn. 27.4.82 'K' LAF, later stored. 3.83 'Z' LAF. 7.83 'BD' 11 Sqn. 12.83. Active 'BD' 11 Sqn 1.84. 22.1.85 St Athan dark grey respray, returned as 'BD' 11 Sqn by 3.85 along with XR773 also coded 'BD', which it replaced 4.85, then stored 5.85. 1.86 'BL' 11 Sqn. 15.7.86 crashed into North Sea seven miles north of Whitby after rear fuselage fire believed caused by fuel leak. Pilot ejected, rescued by 22 Sqn Wessex from Leconfield.

XR761 c/n 95226. f/f 30.9.65 as F3A, Salmesbury-Warton for storage. 15.2.66 'J' 5 Sqn. 23.3.67 60 MU. 5.67 'P' 23 Sqn. 19.1.68 BAC Warton mod to F6. By 10.69 60 MU. 23.10.69 'A' 5 Sqn. 6.70 'B' 74 Sqn. 9.71 'A' 56 Sqn. 6.2.73 60 MU overhaul. 8.6.73 'A' 56 Sqn. 1.7.76 60 MU overhaul. 17.7.76 Binbrook store (26.6.79 painted in 74 Sqn marks for 25th anniversary). 15.8.79 'F' 11 Sqn. 11.80 re-coded 'BF' 11 Sqn. 8.81 St Athan light grey respray. 18.10.81 returned. 2.82 'AC' 5 Sqn. 10.10.83 St Athan dark grey respray returning 8.11.83, into store. 8.11.84 crashed North Sea seven miles east of Spurn Head, after pitch trimmer failure after take-off and then Nos 1 and 2 re-heat fire warning lights came on while pilot burned off fuel preparatory to landing. Smoke and fire caused him to eject — being rescued after 25min in sea.

XR762 c/n 95227. f/f 9.10.65 as F3A, Salmesbury-Warton for storage. 22.2.66 'K' 5 Sqn. 16.1.67 BAC Warton mod to F6 (256hr 29min). 29.12.67 'L' 23 Sqn. 18.2.71 60 MU overhaul. 8.7.71 'H' 11 Sqn. 7.4.75 crashed into sea off Cyprus.

XR763 c/n 95228. f/f 15.10.65 as F3A, Salmesbury-Warton for storage. 11.2.66 'H' 5 Sqn. 3.1.67 BAC, Warton mod to F6. 1.11.67 'G' 23 Sqn. 7.70 'B' 11 Sqn. 14.10.71 60 MU overhaul. 5.72 'B' 11 Sqn. 5.77 store (19.7.79 painted as 'E' 56 Sqn for 25th anniversary). 8.8.79 'E' 11 Sqn. 10.80 re-coded 'BE' 11 Sqn. 4.81 store. 9.11.82 St Athan light grey respray, returning 25.11.82, then 12.82 'AL' 5 Sqn. 1.83 re-coded 'AE' 5 Sqn. 31.1.85 'AN' 5 Sqn. 2.86 store. By 7.5.87 'AP' 5 Sqn. 1.7.87 crashed on approach to Akrotiri during APC after engine flame-out following ingestion of part of target banner. Pilot ejected safely.

XR764 c/n 95229. f/f 4.11.65 as F3A, Salmesbury Warton for storage. 1.3.66 'L' 5 Sqn. 16.3.67 60 MU store. 23.5.67 BAC Warton for mod to F6. 12.7.68 60 MU (278hr 10min). 3.8.68 'P' 5 Sqn. Late 70 'E' 74 Sqn at Tengah. 9.71 'E' 56 Sqn Akrotiri. 30.7.7 crashed into Limasol Bay 29 miles southeast Akrotiri after jet pipe fire. Pilot ejected safely (937hr.)

XR765 c/n 95230. f/f 10.11.65 as F3A, Salmesbury Warton for storage. 8.3.66 'M' 5 Sqn. 24.2.67 BA Warton for mod to F6. 25.3.68 23 Sqn (301hr 41min). 9.8.68 'S' Leuchars Pool (Command Reserve). 2.70 'A' 23 Sqn. 16.8.71 60 MU overhaul 28.1.72 'C' 11 Sqn (loan). 14.2.72 23 Sqn (uncoded) 23.3.73 RAE Bedford (unmarked). 9.10.75 60 MU overhaul. 12.2.76 'C' 11 Sqn. 10.77 store. 11.12.7 'J' 5 Sqn. 8.80 APC Akrotiri, returning as 'E' 5 Sqn then stored 3.9.80. 11.80 'AJ' 5 Sqn. 23.7.81 crashe North Sea 50 miles northeast of Binbrook and 3 miles east of Spurn Head after double reheat fir during Exercise 'Priory', pilot ejected safely Wreckage recovered by Dutch trawler.

XR766 c/n 95231. f/f 11.1.66 as F3A, Salmesbury Warton for storage. 28.3.66 'W' AFDS. By 9.66 'W 5 Sqn marks at Leuchars — believed 'W' Leuchar Pool. 27.7.67 'T' 23 Sqn. 7.9.67 crashed North Se 20 miles east of Montrose after aircraft spun-in Pilot ejected safely. (215hr 15min.)

XR767 c/n 95232. f/f 14.1.66 as F3A, Salmesbury Warton for storage. 31.1.66 'X' 23 Sqn. 30.6.67 'S 23 Sqn. 29.12.67 BAC Warton for mod to F6. 24.1.6 'S' 5 Sqn. 5.70 'E' 74 Sqn Tengah. 26.5.70 crashe into Straits of Malacca off Tengah — caus unknown, only one over-wing tank found.

XR768 c/n 95233. f/f 24.11.65, Salmesbury Warton for storage. 1.8.66 'A' 74 Sqn (first full F6 t RAF). 7.70 60 MU overhaul. 4.71 'P' 5 Sqn. 29.10.7 crashed North Sea three miles off Mablethorp after No 2 engine shut down following possibl reheat fire. Pilot ejected safely. (2,110hr.)

XR769 c/n 95234. f/f 1.12.65, Salmesbury-Warto for storage. 12.9.66 A&AEE. 2.11.66 'B' 74 Sqn 7.2.70 returned to UK from Tengah. 3.70 'S' 5 Sqn mid-70. 60 MU overhaul. 5.71 'J' Sqn. 8.75 store 9.75 loaned 5 Sqn 10.75 'J' 11 Sqn. 17.7.76 store 28.3.78 noted in 5 Sqn marks (uncoded). 7.4.78 'B 11 Sqn (10.7.79 painted as 'B' 19 Sqn for 25t anniversary). 3.8.79 reverted to 'B' 11 Sqn. 10.7 store. 21.7.81 'BB' 11 Sqn. 8.81 re-coded 'BD

Below:
F6 XR753 'A' heads this No 23 Squadron line-up just prior to disbandment in October 1975. No 43's Phantom FG1s and 'Q' sheds are in the background. *Alan Carlaw*

1 Sqn. 7.83 store. 4.84 'BG' 11 Sqn. 2.86 store. 8.86
'BE' 11 Sqn. By 22.7.87 in store. 15.9.87 'AM' 5 Sqn.
remained in use until disbandment 12.87, then
operated, unmarked, by 11 Sqn until 11.4.88 when
it crashed off Humber Estuary following engine
fire; pilot Flt Lt Dick Coleman, Royal Australian AF,
ejected safely.

XR770 c/n 95235. f/f 16.12.65, Salmesbury-
Warton for storage. 9.66 shown SBAC Farnborough
in RSAF marks as '53-770' and flew 10 flights at
show. 26.9.66 'C' 74 Sqn. 14.9.71 60 MU overhaul.
.72 'L' 23 Sqn. 4.3.75 60 MU overhaul. 6.75 'L'
23 Sqn. 9.75 'D' 56 Sqn. 28.6.76 stripped down at
Wattisham. 10.76 moved to Binbrook. 6.78 'B' 5 Sqn.
in storage 6.78 'B' 5 Sqn. 3.79 store. 12.79 'A' 5 Sqn.
.80 'C' 5 Sqn. 9.80 'A' 5 Sqn. 26.11.80 re-coded 'AA'
5 Sqn. 4.81 uncoded. 6.6.81 'AA' 5 Sqn. 15.7.81
St Athan for light grey respray, returning 5.8.81 as
first Lightning in new scheme and over-size
pink/pale blue roundels. 'AA' 5 Sqn. Cat 4 10.81
after u/c damaged in bad landing. 3.83 'X' LAF
(roundels now reduced in size), loaned to 5 Sqn.
7.3.83 for APC, Cyprus. 13.4.83 Binbrook. 7.83 'AA'
5 Sqn. 20.8.84 APC during which 'shark's mouth'
markings applied. 21.1.85 uncoded, placed in store.
1.85 'AJ' 5 Sqn. 1.86 re-coded 'AA' 5 Sqn. 1.10.86
received smaller nose marks, and all-red fin and
maple leaf emblem for 5 Sqn's 21st anniversary
with Lightnings. By 5.10.87 red extended to spine
and wing leading edges. 12.87 following disbandment of 5 Sqn all unit marks removed, fin and
wings painted light grey. By 2.88 fitted with
over-wing tanks and operated (by 11 Sqn) for BAe
Tornado F3 radar development trials from Binbrook. Coded 'BN' 11 Sqn early 4.88, last flight
29.4.88 re-coded 'JS' LTF mid-6.88 for display in
Grimsby. Dismantled.

XR771 c/n 95236. f/f 20.1.66, Salmesbury-Warton
for storage. 20.10.66 'D' 74 Sqn. 9.71 'C' 56 Sqn.
17.5.73 60 MU overhaul. 10.73 Leuchars by 1.75 'C'
56 Sqn. By 11.76 store, Binbrook. 20.11.78 'C' 5 Sqn.
4.80 store. 17.11.80 'AK' 5 Sqn. 3.5.81 store. 1.3.83
'Y' LAF. 8.83 'BA' 11 Sqn. 25.11.83 went u/s
Gütersloh. 15.12.83 returned Binbrook. 4.85 store.
21.3.86 'AN' 5 Sqn. store. XR771. 23.3.88 last flown.
(3,553.55hr.). Salvaged 5.88. 7.88 Midland Air
Museum, Coventry.

XR772 c/n 95237. f/f 10.2.66, Salmesbury-Warton
for storage. 21.10.66 'E' 74 Sqn. 21.1.70 60 MU
overhaul. 3.71 'E' 5 Sqn. 1.11.74 60 MU overhaul.
12.76 'E' 5 Sqn. 1.77 store. 3.10.77 'C' 11 Sqn. 8.78
store. 22.1.81 A&AEE trials, at Binbrook. 3.81 'LTF'
in dayglo on fin. 6.6.81 store, transferred LTF next
day. 8.81 'BB' 11 Sqn. 25.1.83 St Athan for light grey
respray returning 15.2.83, into store. 8.83 'BA'

11 Sqn. 7.84 'AD' 5 Sqn. 6.3.85 crashed North Sea 20
miles northeast of Skegness — entered spin from
11,000ft, possible structural failure. Pilot ejected
safely but was killed when parachute failed to
deploy.

XR773 c/n 95238. f/f 28.2.66, Salmesbury-Warton
for storage. 7.11.66 'F' 74 Sqn. 9.71 'N' 56 Sqn.
13.8.73 60 MU overhaul. 28.1.74 Binbrook. 2.74
returned to 'N' 56 Sqn. 7.75 Binbrook. 2.9.75 'A'
5 Sqn. 16.12.75 recoded 'B' 5 Sqn. 1.76 store. 7.76
'D' 11 Sqn. 11.76 store. 17.1.78 'D' 11 Sqn. 10.78
store. 6.81 'AH' 5 Sqn. 8.82 store. 3.83 'AF' 5 Sqn.
12.83 store. 13.9.84 St Athan for dark grey respray,
returning 9.10.84, into store. 11.84 'BD' 11 Sqn. 3.85
store. 15.5.85 'DF' LTF. 9.1.86 withdrawn from LTF
22.1.86 'AB' 5 Sqn. 9.86 store. By 7.8.87 'BR' 11 Sqn.
Early 88 employed for BAe Tornado F3 radar
development (by 11 Sqn) with over-wing tanks.
27.6.88 Boscombe Down for BAe as spare Tornado
trials a/c.

XS893 c/n 95239. f/f 15.6.66, Salmesbury-Warton
for storage. 23.11.66 'G' 74 Sqn. 12.8.70 crashed in
sea off Tengah when port u/c failed to lower/lock.
Pilot ejected safely, rescued by 103 Sqn Whirlwind
— first night-time helicopter rescue in FEAF.
(857hr 40min.)

XS894 c/n 95240. f/f 18.3.66, Salmesbury-Warton
for storage. 3.1.67 'F' 5 Sqn. 8.9.80 crashed North
Sea five miles off Flamborough Head. USAF
exchange pilot killed. (650hr 45min.)

XS895 c/n 95241. f/f 6.4.66, Salmesbury-Warton
for storage. 5.12.66 'H' 74 Sqn. 8.71 'J' 5 Sqn. 11.71
60 MU overhaul. 24.3.72 'J' 5 Sqn. 24.6.72 re-coded
'B' 5 Sqn. 12.72 'N' 23 Sqn. 15.5.74 'Z' 111 Sqn.
14.10.74 Leuchars Station Flight (operated by
23 Sqn). 11.74 grounded until 2.76. 3.2.76 to
Binbrook, specially decorated in Scottish markings
similar to those of Leuchars TFF. Store. 16.1.79
first flight for three years. 2.79 'B' 5 Sqn. 9.80 'AL'
5 Sqn. 10.81 'AK' 5 Sqn. 6.83 store. 4.84 'DF' LTF.
20.8.84 loaned to 5 Sqn for APC, Cyprus. 29.4.85 on
loan to 11 Sqn. 10.5.85 St Athan for dark grey
respray, returning later same month, into store.
7.85 'BC' 11 Sqn. 15.1.86 slightly damaged after
running off runway. 10.12.86 store. 9.7.87 noted
during overhaul. By 22.8.87 'AO' 5 Sqn, remained
active until disbanded 12.87. Scrapped 4.88.
(3,275hr.)

Below:
**XS903, an F6 of the LTF, is pictured after an emergency nosewheel-up landing at
Coningsby on 14 September 1979. It was a year before it was repaired and back in
service to resume a long career, going on to become the black-finned 'BA' in the closing
months of 11 Squadron's time with Lightnings.** *Via Robin Walker*

XS896 c/n 95242. f/f 25.4.66, Salmesbury-Warton
for storage. 7.12.66 'J' 74 Sqn. 12.9.68 crashed on
approach to Tengah, pilot killed.

XS897 c/n 95243. f/f 10.5.66, Salmesbury-Warton
for storage. 21.12.66 'K' 74 Sqn. 30.8.71 'S' 56 Sqn.
6.9.72 60 MU overhaul. 29.1.73 'S' 56 Sqn via
Binbrook. 7.76 'K' 5 Sqn. 11.76 store. 10.77 'H'
11 Sqn. 3.79 store. 10.4.81 'BE' 11 Sqn. 6.9.81
St Athan for respray, returning 12.10.81. 8.82 store.
2.83 re-coded 'BC' 11 Sqn. 12.83 recoded 'BD'
11 Sqn. 1.84 store. 2.84 'BC' 11 Sqn. 12.84 store.
13.2.86 'AC' 5 Sqn. 10.10.86 old-style camouflage
and 'D' roundels, original 5 Sqn markings as part of
squadron's 21st anniversary of Lightning operations. Remained in this scheme until 5 Sqn
disbanded 12.87 when put into store. Scrapped
4.88. (3,391.55hr.)

XS898 c/n 95244. f/f 20.5.66, Salmesbury-Warton
for storage. 9.1.67 'K' 5 Sqn. 30.1.73 60 MU
overhaul, returned approx 4.73. 17.7.76 store. 6.78
'J' 5 Sqn with experimental unit markings. 2.80
store. 8.80 declared Cat 3 for wing cracks, fuel
leaks and u/c mounting bracket. Airframe severely
overstressed (10G-14G) following pilot disorienta-
tion causing dive at Mach 1.3, but aircraft safely
recovered to Binbrook, where stripped down and
repaired with reinforcing plates! 27.3.81 'BC'
11 Sqn. 3.83 'AK' 5 Sqn. Storage with periodic air
tests until 14.5.86 'BM' 11 Sqn. 7.5.87 store. 29.7.87
'BD' 11 Sqn. 30.6.88 Cranfield for Mr Arnold Glass.

XS899 c/n 95245. f/f 8.6.66, Salmesbury-Warton
for storage. 23.1.67 'G' 5 Sqn. 18.10.73 60 MU
overhaul. 28.1.74 'E' 23 Sqn. 17.7.75 engine runs,
Binbrook. 27.8.75 returned to 'E' 23 Sqn until
disbandment 30.10.75. 3.11.75 Binbrook store. 1.76
noted camouflaged, coded 'W' in black. 24.3.77
flying with 5 Sqn, still coded 'W'. 29.3.77 'L' 5 Sqn.
12.77 store. 4.78 'C' 5 Sqn. 12.78 store. 5.79 'C'
11 Sqn (18.7.79 painted in 92 Sqn markings for 25th
anniversary). 6.8.79 reverted to 'C' 11 Sqn, later
coded 'BC' 11 Sqn. 10.80 store. 3.81 'BL' 11 Sqn. By
10.81 'AA' 5 Sqn. 3.3.82 St Athan for light grey
respray, returning 17.3.82, to 'AA' 5 Sqn. 11.7.83
St Athan for further respray in dark grey, returning
by 8.83. 9.83 store. 4.84 'AJ. 5 Sqn. 11.85 store.
1.10.86 'AM' 5 Sqn. 5.87 store. 7.8.87 lost rudder in

flight due to strong winds, diverted safely to Coningsby. By 10.87 'AF' 5 Sqn until disbandment 12.87 then 'BL' 11 Sqn. 30.6.88 Cranfield for Mr Arnold Glass.

XS900 c/n 95246. f/f 20.6.66, Salmesbury-Warton for storage. 31.1.67 'M' 5 Sqn. 24.1.68 crashed Inchbroom Farm, near Milltown after taking off from Lossiemouth after total loss of power. Pilot ejected successfully.

XS901 c/n 95247. f/f 1.7.66, Salmesbury-Warton for storage. 20.2.67 'D' 5 Sqn. 19.5.70 60 MU overhaul, returned by 6.70. 2.72 'T' 56 Sqn. 1.7.76 60 MU overhaul — final aircraft to pass through 60 MU. 16.11.76 Coningsby store. 5.77 'G' 11 Sqn. 3.79 store. 4.81 'BJ' 11 Sqn. 5.8.81 St Athan for grey/green respray, returning to 'BJ' 1 Sqn by 9.81. 6.83 store. 1.84 'BH' 11 Sqn. 25.9.85 store. 31.7.86 'AH' 5 Sqn, remaining as such until disbanded 12.87. Operated by 11 Sqn coded 'BK' 4.88. 12.5.88 Brüggen, BDR as 8965 M.

XS902 c/n 95248. f/f 14.7.66, Salmesbury-Warton for storage. 1.3.67 'J' 5 Sqn. 25.11.70 60 MU overhaul. 20.5.71 returned to 'J' 5 Sqn. 26.5.71 crashed into North Sea nine miles east of Spurn Head, after reheat fire warnings. (1,051hr.) Pilot ejected safely from 10,000ft.

XS903 c/n 95249. f/f 17.8.66, Salmesbury-Warton for storage. 16.3.67 'A' 5 Sqn (June 69 wore Paris Salon code '91'). 10.69 60 MU overhaul. 10.4.70 seen at Leconfield with black '5' on fin. 4.70 'C' 5 Sqn. 7.1.74 60 MU overhaul. 7.74 returned to 'A' 5 Sqn. 10.76 store. 8.77 'C' 5 Sqn. 4.78 store. 9.79 LTF. 14.9.79 nosewheel-up landing at Coningsby (Cat 4 FA). 8.9.80 returned to Binbrook following repairs. 29.10.80 'BC' 11 Sqn. 3.10.81 store. 16.6.82 St Athan for light grey respray, returning on 12.7.82 to 'BC' 11 Sqn. 6.83 store. 21.8.84 5 Sqn to Akrotiri for APC, coded 'AM' 5 Sqn while there. 10.86 store. By 6.87 'AO' 5 Sqn. By 22.7.87 'BE' 11 Sqn. 4.8.87 lost part of rudder in flight and made emergency landing. By 3.9.87 replaced as 'BE', and by late 11.87 became 'BA' 11 Sqn with black fin and spine. 18.5.88 delivered by CO Wg Cdr Jake Jarron to RAF Elvington for preservation by Yorkshire Air Museum.

XS904 c/n 95250. f/f 26.8.66, Salmesbury-Warton for storage. 18.4.67 'A' 11 Sqn. 11.8.67 60 MU overhaul. 21.12.70 'A' 11 Sqn. 12.70 loaned to 5 Sqn until early 71. 19.8.74 60 MU overhaul. 9.1.75 'A' 11 Sqn, by 7.77 recoded 'B' 11 Sqn. 17.4.78 store. 2.80 'D' 11 Sqn, later 'BD' 11 Sqn. 8.81 store. 5.9.84 'BM' 11 Sqn. 2.1.85 skidded off taxi-way on snow/ice, shearing off nosewheel oleo. Repaired and returned to service as 'BM' by 5.86, when stored.16.3.87 'BQ' 11 Sqn. By 12.87 fitted with over-wing tanks and involved in BAe Tortnado F3 radar development trials (flown by 11 Sqn). 11.4.88 delivered to Warton for BAe continuation of trials. Camouflaged, unmarked. Current 6.88.

XS918 c/n 95251. f/f 22.9.66, Salmesbury-Warton for storage. 14.4.67 'B' 11 Sqn. 4.3.70 crashed, mouth of Firth of Forth near the Isle of May off Leuchars following double reheat fire warning, u/c red light warning and hook-down warning; fire seen in No 1 jetpipe. Pilot ejected safely at 19.00hr but died of exposure having became detached from his survival pack.

XS919 c/n 95252. f/f 28.9.66, Salmesbury-Warton for over-wing tank trials. 14.4.67 'C' 11 Sqn. 2.72 60 MU overhaul. 29.6.72 'R' 56 Sqn. Late 75 60 MU overhaul. 7.76 'C' 5 Sqn. 7.77 re-coded 'A' 5 Sqn. 8.87 re-coded 'F' 5 Sqn. 4.79 store. 13.3.81 'AD' 5 Sqn. Late 82 store. 5.84 'AL' 5 Sqn 3.5.84 St Athan for dark grey respray, returning 30.5.84. 8.6.84 temporarily coded 'AL' 5 Sqn. 11.6.84 stored, then 'BN' 11 Sqn same month. 7.84 store. 2.85 'BN' 11 Sqn. By 20.11.86 'BB' 11 Sqn, last flown 2.88. Salvaged 4.88 (3,987.25hr).

XS920 c/n 95253. f/f 25.10.66, Salmesbury-Warton. 5.12.66 'L' 74 Sqn. 7.70 60 MU overhaul. 11.8.70 'F' 11 Sqn. 19.12.73 60 MU overhaul. 7.74 'E' 11 Sqn, store. 17.7.76 60 MU overhaul. 9.76 Binbrook. 9.77 'E' 11 Sqn. 12.77 store. 21.9.79 'B' 11 Sqn. 10.80 re-coded 'BB' 11 Sqn. 7.81 store. 6.83 St Athan for respray, returning same month, put into store. 11.83 'AF' 5 Sqn. 13.7.84 crashed Heuslingen, 25 miles east of Bremmen, West Germany, while following USAF A-10 at 200ft, hit power cables; pilot killed.

XS921 c/n 95254. f/f 17.11.66, Salmesbury-Warton. 21.12.66 'M' 74 Sqn. 6.9.71 'Q' 56 Sqn. 19.2.74 60 MU overhaul. 2.8.74 'L' 11 Sqn. 11.76 store. 8.10.77 'H' 5 Sqn. 4.78 store. 5.78 'H' 5 Sqn. 11.78 'F' 11 Sqn. 3.82 'AB' 5 Sqn. 12.2.85 St Athan for dark grey respray. 19.3.85 'BA' 11 Sqn. 19.9.85 crashed 17.00hrs 30 miles off Flamborough Head after uncontrolled spin, caused by control column moved fully left, possibly caused by loose article. Pilot ejected successfully.

XS922 c/n 95255. f/f 6.12.66, Salmesbury-Warton. 30.12.66 'H' 5 Sqn. 16.9.70 60 MU overhaul. 28.1.71 'H' 5 Sqn. 15.8.75 60 MU overhaul. 8.1.76 'H' 5 Sqn. 3.76 'P' 56 Sqn. 1.7.76 60 MU overhaul. 17.7.76 Binbrook, placed in store. 18.9.76 'L' 11 Sqn. 11.76 store. 18.2.77 'L' 11 Sqn. 6.79 store. 4.80 'C' 5 Sqn. 8.80 replaced, 9.80 reinstated 'C' 5 Sqn, recoded 11.80 as 'AC' 5 Sqn. 2.82 store. 8.82 'AB' 5 Sqn. 4.83 'BH' 11 Sqn. 6.83 store. Late 83 to BAC Warton. 17.12.83 Binbrook. 9.10.84 St Athan for dark grey respray, returning 26.10.84 into store. 11.84 'AG' 5 Sqn. 5.12.85 nosewheel collapsed on landing at Gütersloh. 19.12.85 returned Binbrook and stored. 7.10.86 'AF' 5 Sqn. Store by 9.87. By 3.88 'BJ' 11 Sqn 5.88 Wattisham BDR.

XS923 c/n 95256. f/f 13.12.66, Salmesbury-Warton. 11.1.67 'M' 5 Sqn. 2.67 re-coded 'C' 5 Sqn. 29.3.70 60 MU overhaul. 7.70 'A' 5 Sqn. 7.74 60 MU overhaul. 1.11.74 'C' 5 Sqn. 7.76 store. 8.78 'J' 11 Sqn. 1.80 store. 8.82 'BG' 11 Sqn. 4.84 store. 21.1.85 'AA' 5 Sqn. 1.86 store. 2.86 'DF' LTF 20.6.86 'BE' 11 Sqn, placed in store after starter explosion. By 9.87 returned to 'BE' 11 Sqn. 30.6.88 Cranfield for Mr Arnold Glass.

XS924 c/n 95257. f/f 11.1.67, Salmesbury-Warton. 24.2.67 'E' 5 Sqn. 29.4.68 crashed Beelsby Farm five miles north of Binbrook during RAF 50th anniversary display while practising AAR (together with XS902 'J') from Victor tanker. It stalled and performed a 'falling leaf' in stream turbulence from the Victor. Pilot killed.

XS925 c/n 95258. f/f 26.1.67, Salmesbury-Warton. 1.3.67 'L' 5 Sqn. 14.9.68 Cat 4 barrier engagement on landing, Binbrook, during Battle of Britain display. 18.11.68 rebuilt by BAc, 24.2.70 f/f after repair. 3.70 'L' 5 Sqn. 28.6.72 60 MU overhaul. 24.10.72 'L' 5 Sqn. 14.8.74 60 MU overhaul. 17.10.74 'L' 5 Sqn. 16.4.75 60 MU overhaul. 21.8.75. 'H' 11 Sqn. 18.9.75 re-coded 'J' 11 Sqn. 10.75 'L' 5 Sqn. 22.4.76 Leconfield. 3.77 Binbrook store. 20.7.79 'D' 5 Sqn. 3.9.80 ex-APC coded 'B' 5 Sqn, but reverted to 'D' 5 Sqn by 10.80. 3.81 store. 10.82 'AD' 5 Sqn. 16.7.84 St Athan for dark grey respray, returning 31.7.84 into store. 21.8.84 coded 'BA' 11 Sqn, port side only, then stored. 2.85 Mod 9 completed to add 400hr to airframe. 5.6.85 'BA' 11 Sqn, re-coded 'BD' 11 Sqn by end 6.85. 3.4.86 lent 5 Sqn for APC, coded 'AP' 5 Sqn. 29.7.87 store. 9.87 withdrawn from use, stripped for spares. 25.4.88 to RAF Museum, Hendon, for display purposes, painted as 'BA', 11 Sqn.

XS926 c/n 95259. f/f 30.1.67, Salmesbury-Warton. 20.3.67 'B' 5 Sqn. 22.9.69 crashed North Sea 51 miles east of Flamborough Head: NO 1 of pair engaged in combat training, when caught in No 2's slipstream, began erratic gyrations, entered spin. USAF pilot ejected safely (703hr 30min.)

XS927 c/n 95260. f/f 15.2.67, Salmesbury-Warton. 3.4.67 'N' 74 Sqn. 14.9.71 60 MU overhaul. 25.5.72 'M' 11 Sqn. 9.72 'O' 23 Sqn. 4.11.75 Binbrook store. 3.76 'G' 5 Sqn. 7.8.76 store. 7.9.79 'H' 11 Sqn, later 'BH' 11 Sqn. 7.11.80 store. 28.10.81 St Athan for respray. 9.12.81 at Binbrook, unmarked, then 'BH' 11 Sqn. 2.83 store. 18.2.85 'BB' 11 Sqn. 26.2.86 returned to Binbrook following diversion to RAF Swinderby a few days earlier. Last flown 10.86; scrapped by 4.88 (3,575.35hr).

XS928 c/n 95261. f/f 28.2.67, Salmesbury-Warton. 4.4.67 'D' 11 Sqn. 1.70. 'L' 74 Sqn. 6.4.70 Cat 4 damage caused by ground fire at Tengah when fuel vented on to wing. 3.11.70 airlifted by Belfast freighter to BAC Warton for repair — new wings fitted (old wings appeared at Gütersloh!). 14.7.72 loaned to 23 Sqn, Leuchars. 16.8.72 'E' 56 Sqn. 4.76 re-coded 'R' 56 Sqn. 1.7.76 60 MU overhaul. 17.7.76 Binbrook store. 9.76 'K' 5 Sqn. By 12.77 'L' 5 Sqn, and by 2.80 'F' 5 Sqn. 10.80 store. 20.10.81 'AJ' 5 Sqn. 6.82 'AU' 5 Sqn. 16.8.82 St Athan for dark grey respray, returning 3.9.82. 5.83 St Athan for further respray, returning 25.5.83 in revised dark grey scheme. 6.83 'BB' 11 Sqn. 5.84 re-coded 'BJ' 11 Sqn. 2.85 Mod 9 completed, adding 400hr to airframe. 2.85 store. 8.85 'AH' 5 Sqn. 7.86 store. 3.87 'AD' 5 Sqn. In use until unit disbanded 12.87 then fitted with over-wing tanks and used in BAe Tornado F3 radar trials. By 4.88 delivered Warton for continuation of trials. Current.

XS929 c/n 95262. f/f 1.3.67, Salmesbury-Warton. 26.4.67 'E' 11 Sqn. 12.1.73 60 MU overhaul. 20.2.73 'E' 11 Sqn. 12.8.73 'L' 56 Sqn. 1.7.76 60 MU overhaul. 17.7.76 Binbrook store. 10.77 'E' 11 Sqn. 8.79 store. 22.1.81 'BF' 11 Sqn, re-coded 'BB' 11 Sqn later. 10.82 'BC' 11 Sqn. 2.83 store. 21.8.85 uncoded with LTF, becoming 'DG' LTF by 6.9.85. 10.4.86 'BG' 11 Sqn. 20.5.88 Akrotiri, gate guardian.

XS930 c/n 95263. f/f 20.3.67, Salmesbury-Warton. 26.5.67 'F' 11 Sqn. 22.5.70 'F' 74 Sqn. 27.7.70 crashed Tengah after climbing too steeply after take-off (which was being filmed), over-rotated at 290kt. Crashed into Malay village killing 2 civilians as well as pilot.

XS931 c/n 95264. f/f 31.3.67, Salmesbury-Warton. 31.5.67 'G' 11 Sqn. 11.8.72 60 MU overhaul. 6.11.72 'G' 11 Sqn. 17.7.76 store. By 12.77 'D' 5 Sqn. 25.5.79 crashed North Sea off Hornsea following control problems. Pilot ejected safely.

XS932 c/n 95265. f/f 9.4.67, Salmesbury-Warton. 21.6.67 'H' 11 Sqn. 14.5.71 60 MU overhaul. 25.10.71 'J' 56 Sqn 25.9.75 60 MU overhaul. 25.2.76 'R' 56 Sqn. 1.7.76 60 MU overhaul. 17.7.76 Binbrook store. By 8.77 Coningsby, stored in BBMF hangar. 4.79 'F' 5 Sqn. 2.80 store. 25.8.83 St Athan for respray in dark grey scheme, returning 12.9.83. 29.9.83 'AM' 5 Sqn. 10.83 re-coded 'AC' 5 Sqn. 4.85 store. 15.1.86 'AG' 5 Sqn. Last flown 10.86 (3,655.30hr). Salvaged 4.88.

XS933 c/n 95266. f/f 27.4.67, Salmesbury-Warton. Loaned to Saudi Training School, Warton. 23.6.67 'J' 11 Sqn. 13.5.71 60 MU overhaul. 14.10.71 'K' 56 Sqn. 7.76 Binbrook store. 28.10.76 transferred to Coningsby store. 5.77 Binbrook store. 9.77 'G' 5 Sqn. 1.78 withdrawn from use. 17.5.78 BAC Warton for instructional use for Saudi Arabian contract. 17.12.82 Binbrook, stored. 6.6.83 St Athan for light grey respray, returning 11.7.83. 9.83 'BE' 11 Sqn. 1.5.85 store. 6.12.85 reported seen as 'BB' 11 Sqn. 15.1.86 'AJ' 5 Sqn, in use until 10.87 then scrapped by 4.88 (3,663.50hr).

XS934 c/n 95267. f/f 11.5.67, Salmesbury-Warton. 3.7.67 'K' 11 Sqn. 19.7.71 60 MU overhaul. 11.71 'J' 5 Sqn. 3.73 'B' 56 Sqn. 3.4.73, crashed two miles off Cyprus following severe vibration and fire, caused by disconnected air trunking. Pilot ejected safely. (1,775hr 30min.)

XS935 c/n 95268. f/f 29.5.67, Salmesbury-Warton. 18.7.67 60 MU store. 1.9.67 Wattisham store. 5.1.68 'J' 23 Sqn. 9.72. 60 MU overhaul. 10.72 'J' 23 Sqn. 22.10.75 Binbrook store. 1.76 'B' 5 Sqn. 7.77 store. 8.80 'J' 5 Sqn. 25.9.80 re-coded 'AB' 5 Sqn. 7.81 store. 9.81 'AB' 5 Sqn. 21.4.82 St Athan for light grey respray, returning 10.5.82 into store. 9.83 'BE' 11 Sqn. 31.7.85 'AK' 5 Sqn. 9.87. Stored. Scrapped 4.88 (3,602.30hr).

XS936 c/n 95269. f/f 31.5.67, Salmesbury-Warton. 27.7.67 60 MU. 18.8.67 'B' 23 Sqn. 28.8.68 to Toronto Air Show in 7hr 20min non-stop. 3.9.68 returned. 26.5.72 60 MU overhaul. 4.9.72 'B' 23 Sqn. 3.11.75 Binbrook store. 21.4.76 60 MU. 7.76 'G' 11 Sqn. 8.77 store. 2.79 'G' 11 Sqn. 9.80 store. 29.4.81 'AK' 5 Sqn. 10.81 'AL' 5 Sqn. 17.3.82 St Athan for light grey respray, returning 1.4.82 into store. 8.82 'DF' LTF. 7.4.83 'Pool' aircraft. 5.83 'L' 5 Sqn. 12.83 'DF' LTF, replaced by 4.84. 17.5.85 'AS' 5 Sqn. By 25.9.87 'AB' 5 Sqn. Last flown 10.87. Scrapped 4.88 (3,961.50hr).

XS937 c/n 95270. f/f 26.6.67, Salmesbury-Warton. 21.7.67 60 MU 21.8.67 'C' 23 Sqn. 4.9.72 60 MU overhaul. 6.6.73 'C' 23 Sqn. 12.75 loaned 56 Sqn, then returned Binbrook. 2.76 'M' 11 Sqn. 4.76 re-coded 'K' 11 Sqn. 30.7.76 crashed off Flamborough Head when starboard u/c failed to lower, trailed at 20°. Pilot ejected safely at 7,000ft and 300kt.

XS938 c/n 95271. f/f 30.6.67, Salmesbury-Warton. 28.8.67 'E' 23 Sqn. 28.4.71 crashed in River Tay estuary folowing re-heat fire. Pilot ejected safely. (1,233hr 45min.)

LIGHTNING F52

52-655 (ex-XN767). 22.7.66, to Saudi Arabia. 7.8.67 re-serialled 52-609. 6 Sqn. Displayed, camouflaged, on plinth, Dhahran.

52-656 (ex-XN770). 11.7.66 to Saudi Arabia. 7.8.67 re-serialled 52-610. 6 Sqn. Static Display status by 1981, at Riyadh.

52-657 (ex-XN796). 18.7.66 to Saudi Arabia, but delivery delayed by brake chute failure at Muharraq. 6 Sqn. 20.9.66 Crashed on take-off from Mushayt, and written off.

52-658 (ex-XN797). 22.7.66 to Wattisham for delivery to Saudi Arabia. 6 Sqn, re-serialled 52-611. 28.11.68 crashed while practising single engine approaches to Khamis Mushayt.

52-659 (ex-XN729). 10.5.67 to Saudi Arabia. Re-serialled 52.612. 2.5.70 crashed near Kharmis Mushayt.

LIGHTNING F53

53-666 c/n 95205. ex-XR722 (F6). f/f 23.1.65. Modified to F53 and f/f as such 19.10.66 serialled G-27-2. 28.8.69 RSAF; served with 1 Sqn, 2 Sqn ('201'). 6.2.72 crashed while on loan to 6 Sqn (364hr).

53-667 c/n 95272. f/f 13.7.67 (G-27-37). 20.9.68 to RSAF, served with 2 Sqn ('202'), 13 Sqn (1301), 2 Sqn ('221'). 3.9.85 crashed 28 miles north of Tabuk after reheat fire.

53-668 c/n 95273. f/f 4.9.67 (G-27-38). 8.11.68 to RSAF; served with 6 Sqn, 2 Sqn ('201', then 'A'). 14.1.86 returned to Warton from Tabuk, non-stop as ZF577 (2,071.36hr).

53-669 c/n 95274. f/f 12.9.67 (G-27-39). 11.10.68 to RSAF; served as reserve a/c, stored at Riyadh for much of its life. 21.4.79 crashed near Tabuk after running out of fuel.

53-670 c/n 95275. f/f 12.10.67 (G-27-40). 8.11.68 to RSAF, Jeddah. Served with 2 Sqn ('202', then 'B'). 14.1.86 returned to Warton from Tabuk as ZF578 (1,886.18hr).

53-671 c/n 95276. f/f 2.11.67 (G-27-41). 11.10.68 to RSAF, Jeddah. Served with 2 Sqn ('203', then 'C'). 14.1.86 returned to Warton from Tabuk as ZF579 (2,119.42hr).

53-672 c/n 95277. f/f 28.11.67 (G-27-42). 18.11.68 to RSAF, Jeddah. Served with LCU, 2 Sqn ('204', then 'D'). 14.1.86 returned to Warton from Tabuk as ZF580 (2,304.54hr).

53-673 c/n 95278. f/f 4.12.67 (G-27-43). 23.8.68 to RSAF, Jeddah. Served as '302', then 2 Sqn ('205'). 22.9.80 collided with 53-680 and crashed, Khamis Mushayt.

53-674 c/n 95279. f/f 12.12.67 (G-27-44). 18.11.68 to RSAF Jeddah. Served with LCU, 2 Sqn ('205'). 28.9.72 crashed off Bahrain.

53-675 c/n 95280. f/f 19.12.67 (G-27-45). 16.9.68 to RSAF, Jeddah. Served with 2 Sqn ('206' then 'E'). 14.1.86 returned to Warton from Tabuk as ZF581 (1,972.42hr).

53-676 c/n 95281. f/f 15.1.68 (G-27-46). 20.9.68 to RSAF, Jeddah. Served with 2 Sqn ('210', then 'G' then '207', then 'F'). 22.1.86 returned to Warton from Tabuk as ZF582 (1,881.24hr).

53-677 c/n 95282. f/f 31.1.68 (G-27-47). 23.7.68 to RSAF, Jeddah. Served with 2 Sqn ('208'). 4.9.83 crashed at night.

53-678 c/n 95283. f/f 13.2.68 (G-27-48). last F53 built at Samlesbury. 23.8.68 to RSAF, Jeddah. 21.4.79 crashed during sandstorm after running out of fuel.

53-679 c/n 95284. f/f 4.3.68 (G-27-49). 16.9.68 to RSAF, Jeddah. Served with 2 Sqn ('206'); 6 Sqn, 13 Sqn ('1302'), 2 Sqn ('220', then 'S'). 22.1.86 returned to Warton from Tabuk, as ZF590 (2,281.36hr).

53-680 c/n 95285. f/f 18.3.68. (G-27-50). 23.7.68 to RSAF, Jeddah. Served with 6 Sqn ('305'). 22.9.80 destroyed in collision with 53-673.

53-681 c/n 95286. f/f 28.3.68 (G-27-51). 1.7.68 to RSAF, Jeddah. Served with 6 Sqn ('306'), 2 Sqn ('210', then 'H'). 14.1.86 returned to Warton from Tabuk as ZF583 (1,885.14hr).

53-682 c/n 95287. f/f 5.4.68 (G-27-52). 1.7.68 to RSAF, Jeddah. Served with 6 Sqn ('307'). 2 Sqn ('211', then 'J'). 22.1.86 returned to Warton from Tabuk, as ZF584 (1,975hr).

53-683 c/n 95288. f/f 23.4.68 (G-27-53). 11.3.69 to RSAF. Served with LCU, 2 Sqn ('207', then '212', then 'K'). 14.1.86 returned to Warton from Tabuk as ZF585 (2,052.18hr).

53-684 c/n 95289. f/f 10.5.68 (G-27-54). 18.11.68 to RSAF, Jeddah. Served with LCU, 2 Sqn ('208'), 13 Sqn ('1303'). 30.6.80 crashed on take-off from Dhahran.

53-685 c/n 95290. f/f 29.5.68 (G-27-55). 31.1.69 to RSAF. Served with LCU, 2 Sqn ('209'), 13 Sqn ('1304'), 2 Sqn ('222', then 'U'). 14.1.86 returned to Warton from Tabuk as ZF591 (2,110.24hr).

53-686 c/n 95291. f/f 11.6.68 (G-27-56). Shown as G-AWON at 9.68 SBAC show. 16.4.69 to RSAF, Jeddah. Served with LCU, 2 Sqn ('201'), 13 Sqn ('1305'), 2 Sqn ('223', then 'V'). 22.1.86 returned to Warton as ZF592 (2,297.12hr).

53-687 c/n 95293. f/f 5.7.68 (G-27-57). 9.68 allocated G-AWOO at SBAC show. 17.4.69 to RSAF, Jeddah. Served with LCU, 2 Sqn ('F'), LCU, 13 Sqn ('1306'), 2 Sqn ('224'). Withdrawn from use, Tabuk, approx late 84.

53-688 c/n 95294. f/f 12.7.68 (G-27-58). 16.4.69 to RSAF, Jeddah. Served with LCU, 6 Sqn, 2 Sqn, ('213', then 'L'). 22.1.86 returned to Warton as ZF586 (1,938.48hr).

53-689 c/n 95295. f/f 17.7.68 (G-27-59). 18.11.68 to RSAF, Jeddah. Served with 2 Sqn ('J', then '214'). 27.7.84 crashed Tabuk (1781.12hr).

53-690 c/n 95296. f/f 20.8.68 (G-27-60). 4.9.68 crashed, Pilling, Lancs, on fourth flight, from Warton, after total control failure.

53-691 c/n 95297. f/f 29.8.68 (G-27-61). 31.1.69 to RSAF, Jeddah. Served with 2 Sqn ('N'). 22.1.86 returned to Warton as ZF587. (1,947.24hr).

53-692 c/n 95298. f/f 24.9.68 (G-27-62). 17.4.69 to RSAF, Jeddah. Served with 6 Sqn (experimental camouflage, coded 'L'), 13 Sqn ('1307'), 2 Sqn ('225', then 'X'). 22.1.86 returned the Warton as ZF 593 (2,130.06hr).

53-693 c/n 95300. f/f 9.10.68 (G-27-63). 23.5.69 to RSAF, Jeddah. Served with 2 Sqn ('L'), LCU, 2 Sqn ('216', then 'O'). 14.1.86 returned to Warton as ZF588 (2,005.12hr).

53-694 c/n 95301. f/f 17.10.68 (G-27-66). 3.6.69 to RSAF, Jeddah. Served at Khamis Mushayt and Dhahran, latterly with LCU. 11.9.76 crashed near Khamis after spin.

53-695 c/n 95302. f/f 30.10.68 (G-27-65). 23.5.69 to RSAF, Jeddah. Served with 6 Sqn, 2 Sqn ('M' and '217'). 28.9.81 Destroyed Tabuk on training sortie.

53-696 c/n 95303. f/f 14.11.68 (G-27-66). 3.6.69 to RSAF, Jeddah. Served with LCU, 13 Sqn ('1308'), 2 Sqn ('226' and 'Y'). 14.1.86 returned to Warton as ZF584 (2,057.06hr).

53-697 c/n 95304. f/f 29.11.68 (G-27-67). 26.8.69 to RSAF, Jeddah. 30.5.70 crashed near Yemeni border during reconnaissance after being hit by ground fire.

53-698 c/n 95305. f/f 11.12.68 (G-27-6?). 3.6.69 to RSAF, Jeddah. Served with 2 Sqn, LCU, 13 Sqn ('1309'), 2 Sqn ('219'). Withdrawn approx 84.

53-699 c/n 95306. f/f 23.12.68 (G-27-6?). 3.6.69 to RSAF, Jeddah. Served with 6 Sqn, 13 Sqn ('1310') 2 Sqn ('227'). 8.85 installed on plinth at Tabuk, by BAe.

53-700 c/n 95317. f/f 29.7.72 (G-27-223). Last production Lightning, partly built from end-of-line components, to replace 53-690. 4.9.72 to RSAF. Served with 6 Sqn, 2 Sqn ('218', then 'Q'). 14.1.86 returned to Warton as ZF589 (2,045.06hr).

53-412 c/n 95292. f/f 21.6.68 (G-27-80). 18.12.68 to Kuwait AF. Coded 'C'. Stored early 80s.

53-413 c/n 95299. f/f 13.9.68 (G-27-81). 25.3.69 to Kuwait AF. Coded 'E' Soc in 75.

53-414 c/n 95307. f/f 12.11.68 (G-27-82). 25.3.69 to Kuwait AF. Code 'F' 10.4.71 crashed after fire.

53-415 c/n 95308. f/f 12.2.69 (G-27-83). 23.5.69 to Kuwait AF. Coded 'H'.

53-416 c/n 95309. f/f 25.2.69 (G-27-84). 11.7.69 to Kuwait AF. Coded 'J'. Stored 69.

53-417 c/n 95310. f/f 14.3.69 (G-27-85). 23.5.69 to Kuwait AF. Coded 'K'.

53-418 c/n 95311. f/f 25.4.69 (G-27-86). 6.69 at Paris Salon coded '512' and G-AXEE. 11.7.69 to Kuwait AF. Coded 'L'.

53-419 c/n 95312. f/f 20.5.69 (G-27-87). Registration allocated G-AXFW. 26.8.69 to Kuwait AF. Coded 'M'. 2.8.71 crashed, Rezayat, on take-off (84.15hr).

53-420 c/n 95313. f/f 8.5.69 (G-27-88). 19.7.69 to Kuwait AF. Coded 'N'. Crashed.

53-421 c/n 95314. f/f 18.6.69 (G-27-89). 19.7.69 to Kuwait AF. Coded 'O'.

53-422 c/n 95315. f/f 18.8.69 (G-27-90). 4.12.69 to Kuwait AF. Coded 'P'.

53-423 c/n 95316. f/f 11.9.69 (G-27-91). 3.12.69 to Kuwait AF. Coded 'R'.

Above right:
No 2 Sqn markings and number of the fin of 53-679 '206' at Dhahran in 1970.

Below:
Royal Saudi AF Lightning F53 53-685 '209' of No 2 Squadron at Dhahran, complete with practice bombs on the under-wing pylons.

LIGHTNING T54

54-650 c/n 95077. (ex-XM989). 7.4.66 delivered Warton for conversion to T54. 6.6.66 to RSAF. 6 Sqn at Riyadh; later used for ground instruction. Displayed Dhahran. (Re-serialled 54.067).

54-651 c/n 95080 (ex-XM992). 12.4.66 delivered Warton for conversion to T54. 6.6.66 to RSAF, later re-serialled 54-608. 26.10.70 starter fire at Khamis caused a/c to be written off.

LIGHTNING T55

55-710 c/n 95020 (ex-XS460). f/f 2.2.66. First T55 7.3.67 crashed on landing at Warton in strong cross wind (14.53hr).

55-711 c/n 95024. f/f 29.8.67 (G-27-70). 2.2.68 Coltishall for Saudi pilot training coded 'A'/'203'. 27.8.69 to RSAF, Jeddah. Re-serialled 55-71. Served LCU, 6 Sqn, 13 Sqn ('1315'), 2 Sqn ('234'), 14.1.86 returned to Warton as ZF597 (2,484.48hr).

55-712 c/n 95025. f/f 12.10.67 (G-27-71). 15.2.68 Colitshall, coded 'B'/'207'. 11.7.69 to RSAF, Jeddah. Served with LCU, 6 Sqn. 21.5.74 crashed into Half Moon Bay.

55-713 c/n 95026. f/f 16.11.67 (G-27-72). 2.2.68 Coltishall, coded 'C'/'206'. 27.8.69 to RSAF, Jeddah. Served with LCU, 6 Sqn, 13 Sqn ('1316'), 2 Sqn ('235'). 14.1.86 returned to Warton from Tabuk as ZF598 (2,233.30hr).

55-714 c/n 95027. f/f 1.2.68 (G-27-73). 22.3.68 Coltishall, coded 'D'/'212'. 11.7.69 to RSAF, Jeddah. Served with LCU, 6 Sqn, 13 sqn ('1317'), 2 Sqn ('231'). 22.1.86 returend to Warton as ZF595

Above:
Royal Saudi AF Lightning T55s 716 and 711 of the LCU at Dhahran in 1970.

(2,370.06hr).

55-715 c/n 95028. f/f 28.2.68 (G-27-74). 11.3.69 to RSAF. Served LCU, 6 Sqn ('305'/'205'), 2 Sqn ('220'/'233'). 22.1.86 returned to Warton as ZF596 (2,053.12hr).

55-716 c/n 95030. f/f 14.7.69 (G-27-75). 30.9.69 to RSAF. Served LCU ('E'), 2 Sqn ('219'/'230'). Grounded 7.84.

55-410 c/n 95023. f/f 24.5.68 (G-27-78). 30.9.69 to Kuwait AF. Coded 'A'.

55-411 c/n 95029. f/f 3.4.69 (G-27-79). 3.12.69 to Kuwait AF. Coded 'B'.

ADDITIONAL INFORMATION

Ex-Saudi Lightnings held in store at Warton since their return to the UK in December 1986 are being disposed of to preservation groups/museums, and to salvage dealers. One F53 will be retained by British Aerospace as a gate guardian at Warton.

RAF gate guardian Lightnings are under threat as a consequence of MoD policy to limit historic aircraft to one per base for such display purposes; among the airframes currently threatened with disposal and probable destruction is the 'Airfix' Lightning F1A, XM192, formerly 'K' of No 111 Squadron at RAF Wattisham.

The three ex-RAF Lightning F6s currently operated, together with XP693, by BAer on Tornado F3 development work, are now expected to remain active until late 1990.

The very last RAF Lightning sortie was flown by Sqn Ldr John Aldington, the last CO of No 11 (Lightning) Squadron, when he delivered F6 XS923 'BE' to Cranfield on 30 June 1988.

Airframe hours of preserved Lightning F6 XR 728 'JS' at Bruntingthorpe are 3,708.

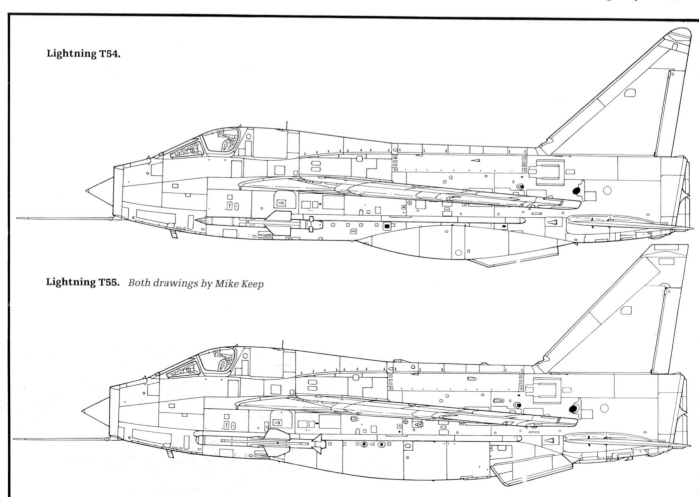

Lightning T54.

Lightning T55. *Both drawings by Mike Keep*